Nicaragua:
What went wrong?

This book is published with the aid of the Bookmarks Publishing Co-operative. Many socialists have some savings put aside, probably in a bank or savings bank. While there, this money is being loaned out by the bank to some business or other to further the capitalist search for profit. We believe it is better loaned to a socialist venture to further the struggle for socialism. That's how the co-operative works: in return for a loan, repayable at a month's notice, members receive free copies of books published by Bookmarks. At the time this book was published, the co-operative had 400 members, from as far apart as London and Malaysia, Canada and Norway. Since 1980, the co-operative has helped publish more than fifty books.
Like to know more? Write to the Bookmarks Publishing Co-operative, 265 Seven Sisters Road, Finsbury Park, London N4 2DE, England.

Bookmarks
London, Chicago and Melbourne

Nicaragua:
What went wrong?

Mike Gonzalez

with a report from Managua
by Sabby Sagall

Nicaragua: What went wrong? / *Mike Gonzalez*
First published April 1990.
Bookmarks, 265 Seven Sisters Road, London N4 2DE, England
Bookmarks, PO Box 16085, Chicago, IL 60616, USA
Bookmarks, GPO Box 1473N, Melbourne 3001, Australia
Copyright © Bookmarks and Mike Gonzalez
Editor's note: Parts of this book first appeared as **Nicaragua:
Revolution under siege** (Bookmarks 1985) and as articles in
International Socialism journal. Full sources are given in the text.

ISBN 0 906224 59 4

Printed by Cox and Wyman Limited, Reading, England
Cover design by Peter Court

Bookmarks is linked to an international grouping of socialist organisations:
Australia: *International Socialists,* GPO Box 1473N, Melbourne 3001
Belgium: *Socialisme International,* Rue Lovinfosse 60, 4030 Grivegnée
Britain: *Socialist Workers Party,* PO Box 82, London E3
Canada: *International Socialists,* PO Box 339, Station E, Toronto,
        Ontario M6H 4E3
Denmark: *Internationale Socialister,* Ryesgade 8, 3, 8000 Århus C
France: *Socialisme International,* BP 189, 75926 Paris Cedex 19
Greece: *Organosi Sosialistiki Epanastasi,* PO Box 8161, 10010 Omonia,
        Athens.
Holland: *Groep Internationale Socialisten,* PO Box 9720, 3506 GR Utrecht
Ireland: *Socialist Workers Movement,* PO Box 1648, Dublin 8
Norway: *Internasjonale Sosialister,* Postboks 5370, Majorstua, 0304 Oslo 3
United States: *International Socialist Organization,* PO Box 16085,
        Chicago, IL 60616
West Germany: *Sozialistische Arbeiter Gruppe,* Wolfgangstrasse 81, 6000
        Frankfurt 1

Contents

Map 1:
Central America

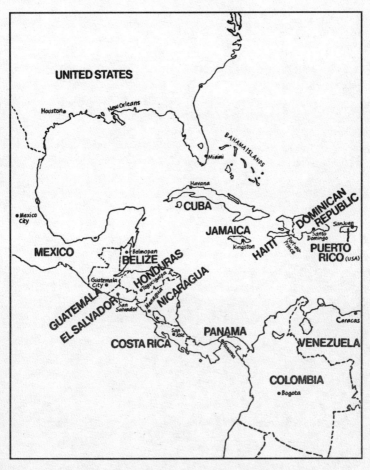

Map 2:
Nicaragua

Acknowledgements

Anyone who writes on Central America owes an incalculable debt to Jenny Pearce. I am one of them.

Authors

Mike Gonzalez is a lecturer in Hispanic Studies at the University of Glasgow and the author of **Cuba, Castro and socialism** (1983, with Peter Binns)and **Nicaragua: Revolution under Siege** (1985). He visited Nicaragua in 1982 and Mexico in 1986.

Sabby Sagall taught Sociology at the Polytechnic of East London and is now a full-time writer. He was in Nicaragua during summer 1989.

Both are members of the Socialist Workers Party in Britain

Chapter one
The impact of an election

THE defeat of the Sandinista government of Nicaragua in the elections of February 1990—an election result in a small Central American country of only three million people, of little strategic importance and little economic power—had an impact around the world of extraordinary dimensions. In the elections a coalition of right-wing organisations, UNO, won an overwhelming victory. They received 54.7 per cent of the vote to the Sandinistas' 40.8 per cent, giving them 51 seats in the National Assembly to the Sandinistas' 39 seats.

Immediately every newspaper headline writer and television commentator pronounced the Nicaraguan revolution dead. The Contras, the death squads of El Salvador, US president George Bush and British prime minister Margaret Thatcher united in celebrating the Sandinistas' fall, which was portrayed as the latest defeat for 'Marxists' at the hands of the very people they supposedly represented.

And there is no avoiding it; a significant proportion of those who voted in the right-wing coalition of UNO were the same people who, eleven years earlier, had carried the Sandinistas into the Nicaraguan capital, Managua, at the head of a great insurrectionary demonstration. In July 1979 those same people, with the Sandinistas at their head, had overthrown a dictatorship of peculiar brutality and stability. With little in the way of resources, few political traditions, and a political leadership that was not only inexperienced but also completely unprepared to the lead the insurrection, they had overthrown the dictatorship of the Somoza family, a tyranny that had lasted 43 years and looked set to be there forever.

It had been a mass, popular revolution. Of that too there is no doubt. Fifty thousand Nicaraguans died in the struggle to remove Anastasio Somoza, whose armed forces bombed hospitals and factories and whose National Guard tortured and killed thousands in an attempt to break the mass movement that opposed them. The Sandinistas, when they took over, proclaimed a new society—which was to be a model of equality and mass democracy. The urban *barrios*, the poor working-class districts, celebrated what they saw as their collective power by tearing down the statue of Somoza outside the stadium in Managua. Mass involvement in the dictator's overthrow pointed to the potential for mass revolutionary organisation.

When the Sandinistas, the FSLN, stood nearly eleven years later in the elections of 25 February 1990, they did so as the self-proclaimed representatives of that mass movement. The banner of the FSLN had led the victorious march into Managua on 19 July 1979, and it was the FSLN that in the intervening years were presented to the world as the inheritors of that revolution. Several surveys indicated that the FSLN would win the elections quite comfortably. Similar surveys just over a year earlier had shown Sandinista support to be waning rapidly—even the FSLN acknowledged as much--but that was forgotten in the pre-election euphoria.

How, then, did they lose? Who defeated them? What interests were represented by the UNO coalition?

UNO was formed in June 1985, at the insistence of the United States. As US strategy shifted towards a combined military, economic and political assault on Nicaragua, UNO was to represent the 'internal front', the political weapon. It was formed from an uneasy combination of right-wing organisations and individuals, supporters of the Contra guerrilla movement and of the business organisation COSEP, which had coordinated political opposition to the Sandinistas from the outset. The church hierarchy, under the newly promoted Cardinal Miguel Obando y Bravo, was an active organising focus for the 'internal front'; lest there was any doubt about where the new cardinal stood, he celebrated his first mass as Nicaragua's chief religious leader not in Managua, but in Miami, among the active supporters and organisers of the Contras.

This left little doubt as to what was meant by the 'national reconciliation' set out in UNO's founding programme.[1] Essentially, UNO was the new face of the counter-revolution, remodelled after the US had failed to prevent the Nicaraguan presidential election of 1984 giving the FSLN an overwhelming victory and after the lack of Contra military success. Its figurehead, and presidential candidate in the elections of 1990, was a woman whom the press had suddenly started describing as a 'white-haired widow of sixty': Violeta Chamorro, the widow of the newspaper editor Pedro Joaquin Chamorro, who had been killed by Somoza in January 1978.

Chamorro, editor of *La Prensa*, had been a bitter opponent of Somoza. But he was not an opponent from the left; he belonged to a group of bankers, financiers and industrialists who felt that they were not getting an adequate or equal share of the cake that Somoza was greedily keeping to himself. Their opposition came to a head particularly when the 1972 earthquake produced millions of dollars in aid for Nicaragua, all of which went into the pockets of Somoza and his immediate supporters. Among the group around Chamorro there were few voices saying 'This is a disgrace. This aid is intended to save the poorest and weakest parts of the population.' There were many letters and newspaper articles, however, saying 'What about a bit for us?' That, essentially, was the line that Chamorro took.

Chamorro was a lifelong conservative, and his opposition to Somoza was a squabble within the capitalist family. But he *was* a fierce opponent, and in the absence of any voices from the left he became popularly identified with opposition to Somoza. When he was murdered on Somoza's orders, his funeral sparked a mass protest movement, beginning in the poorest quarters of the town of Masaya, 40 kilometres from Managua. That day in Masaya, in January 1978, the insurrection began that 18 months later overthrew Somoza.

The insurrection began in the poorest quarter of Masaya, Monimbo, not because Chamorro led it or had called for it, but because his murder crystallised the tyranny of Somoza in the minds of the people. There was another deeper reason for the insurrection too: 1978 was when a deepening world recession hit Nicaragua hardest, because it was amongst the world's poorest countries, where the effects of the recession bit so deep that the poorest and weakest sections of the population were driven to rise up in resistance.

Immediately after July 1979 Violeta Chamorro ceased to be a liberal democrat. She became a bitter opponent of the Sandinista regime. *La Prensa* was not a liberal, socially aware newspaper, concerned for the rights of ordinary people. It was a savagely anti-Sandinista newspaper, which published, day after day, scare stories about the economy, denunciations of peasants who took over land, of workers who went on strike, continually emphasising tragedies and disasters in order to create an atmosphere of insecurity and distress. This is what Violeta Chamorro represented in her leadership of UNO.

The press made great play of describing UNO as 'a coalition of parties of the far left and the far right'. That can be dismissed very quickly. There were two 'far-left' parties. The PSN, the Socialist Party of Nicaragua, was the 'official' Communist Party. Like most of the other official Communist parties of the world, it had decided that workers' power was a terrible idea and had moved with dramatic speed to the right. Perhaps this is not surprising, since the PSN was actually founded by Somoza; at its opening rally in 1944 the back of the stage was decorated with his huge portrait. The other 'far-left' party, the Stalinist PCN, was formed by a group who split from the PSN precisely because it had entered a tactical alliance with the FSLN in 1978. The PCN had no international connections.

These two parties, whose hatred of the Sandinistas and whose unprincipled opportunism led them into a coalition with parties they knew perfectly well to be the extreme right, could hardly claim to represent any left-wing forces—and they certainly didn't.[2] Alongside them in UNO were members of various conservative parties, including the Independent Liberal Party (PLI), whose leader Virgilio Godoy was UNO's vice-presidential candidate—and who had been recently exposed for making a private fortune out of US political funding for his organisation. Apart from the PSN and PCN, the other twelve organisations were a variety of right-wing groups linked or sympathetic to the Contras. In some ways UNO was the internal front, the Contras the external expression of a single strategy.

That strategy was directly orchestrated by the US government under president Ronald Reagan. For he and his foreign policy advisors placed Nicaragua at the centre of their project to overcome the 'Vietnam syndrome' and put the United States back at the head of the global system. That policy, set out in the so-called Santa Fé Letter of 1980, declared that 'war and not peace is the norm in international affairs'. The Committee on the Present Danger, formed four years earlier, gathered the gamut of right- wing ideas under the umbrella of a single objective: to reconstitute the imperialist role of the United States. These ideologues were quick to recognise that one revolution can easily lead to another, and saw the destruction of Nicaragua as an essential first step in rolling back the revolutionary tide.

Their chosen instrument for this task, once Reagan was in power, was the Contras. As early as March 1981, the Reagan administration had taken the decision to provide funds and support for the groups of former members of Somoza's National Guard then living in exile in Honduras, close to the border with Nicaragua. From there they were conducting raids across the frontier and terrorising the local population. A first group was taken for training to Panama, and there placed under the command of Enrique Bermúdez, once Nicaraguan military attaché in Washington, and Ricardo 'El Chino' Lau, whose sadistic reputation was thoroughly deserved. Both were already in the pay of the CIA. Other former Somocista groups that had fled the revolution, including one led by Somoza's son, were drawn together under US patronage to form the UDN, the 'National Democratic Front'.

In mid-1982, with 6000 or so people under arms, the assault on Nicaragua began. The attacks escalated through 1982 and 1983. They all bore what was to become the particular trademark of Contra attacks: their victims were horribly tortured, then mutilated in particularly sadistic ways. The dismembered bodies were then left in public places to terrify and terrorise the local population. In 1985 the US magazine **Newsweek** carried a series of photographs showing how the Contras conducted their killings. Despite the dewy-eyed plaudits handed to them by the US administration and Congressional spokespersons, their role has remained the same. Only days before the elections of 1990, the Contras left their latest victims, workers and peasants, horribly murdered by the roadside.

By late 1984 the Contras claimed a membership of 20,000. There was ample evidence to show, however, that their recruitment methods were based on kidnapping and dire threats. While US policy after 1984 tended to shift the emphasis from a military to a combined 'low-intensity' strategy of economic and political aggression supported and reinforced by military actions, US material and financial support for the Contras flowed without interruption. The Contras, therefore, made no change in their methods of operation.[3]

The Contras were sadistic murderers whose job was not simply to kill people, but to destabilise and undermine the Nicaraguan economy and Nicaraguan society in two parallel ways. First by making the economy unworkable, largely by border raids, burning coffee fields or terrorising the peasantry in order to stop not only the harvesting of coffee, which would then die on the trees, but also its replanting. Secondly, the Contra terror was itself a political instrument. The evidence of its success was a mounting refugee population: over the four years after 1985 roughly half a million people fled from the border areas and towards Managua. In a country of around three million people, that in itself caused considerable economic problems.

In the weeks and months before the 1990 elections, those who spoke on behalf of the UNO coalition and on behalf of the US government absolutely denied any connection between UNO and the Contras. However, a widely publicised letter from Alfredo Cesar, one of Violeta Chamorro's immediate allies, to the head of the Contras, General Bermúdez, made the connection clear. Cesar asked Bermúdez: 'Please under no circumstances disband the Contra forces or cease your military activity until the elections are over.'

Violeta Chamorro herself, despite a sequence of increasingly horrible murders by the Contras in the twelve months up to the elections, never once publicly opposed Contra activity. *La Prensa* had been a consistent champion of the Contra cause from the moment they were formed. Only in the wake of her victory did she announce that she was 'uneasy' about Contra activity. Like her colleagues she was happy to exploit the effects of Contra activity during the election campaign.

The Contras were the iron fist, UNO the velvet glove. Both represented the bourgeoisie, which, inside and outside Nicaragua, had since 1979 seen it as its class purpose to undermine and destroy the Nicaraguan revolution. This was not specialised knowledge; this was not knowledge which comes from reading between the lines of recondite and obscure American journals; the activities and connections of those who led UNO were well-known in Nicaragua before the elections. Their political credentials were clear.

What then caused the people of Nicaragua, including many workers, knowing exactly who UNO were, to vote for them?

The simplest answer to this question is poverty, a catastrophic decline in the standard of living of most Nicaraguans. By the beginning of 1990 the purchasing power and the real value of wages in Nicaragua was below that of 1979. In 1988 inflation reached an astonishing 35,000 per cent. The wage you had in December bought you less than a tenth of what it would have bought in the previous January. It meant that people were hungry. It meant that people were going without absolute essentials for months at a time.

Not only that, but the economic situation meant that the aims that had been inscribed on the banners of the revolution in 1979: health, education, housing—the foundations of a minimal welfare state that had been laid in the two years that followed—were slashed and slashed again. And they were cut not just in the final months before the elections of February 1990, but again and again in the years after 1982.

The austerity programme of 1988, which cut public spending to an absolute minimum, was only the last in a series of steps. Some tragic statistics emerged from it. For example illiteracy, in 1980-81, had been cut to 12 per cent in a wonderful and inspiring literacy campaign that all the world spoke about. By 1990 illiteracy was back up again, beyond 30 per cent. Infant mortality, perhaps the most poignant and central measure of a developing health system, rose again after 1986, when it had been progressively reduced in the first five years of the decade.

Against this background, a general disillusionment would hardly be surprising. To add to this there was war-weariness. More than 40,000 people had died in the fighting against the Contras. In a country of three million this meant that every family had someone who had been killed, wounded, or who was crippled for life as a result of the war against the Contras. Of the national budget for 1989, 62.5 per cent went on defence spending—at the expense, inevitably, of the social gains of the revolution.

The Contras alone had not been the cause of this. Without the backing of the United States, they would have remained an exiled and disaffected minority. But the Contras were guaranteed funds from the US. Much of this came from the president's Special Contingency Fund and courtesy of the 'Contragate' operation —the process by which undercover funds derived from secret arms sales to Iran were passed on to the Contras without the knowledge of Congress, and often contrary to its stated policies. In any event, Congress could always be persuaded to vote aid to the Contras by some well-placed rumours about Russian or Cuban involvement in Nicaragua. Millions of dollars of US aid thus supported the Contra campaign of murder and destruction.

The other side of this coin was that the US used its economic power to isolate Nicaragua from potential sources of outside support. The US used its veto in the world's international aid agencies to ensure that the usual aid available to the world's poorer countries was cut off. After 1984 there was no international aid available to Nicaragua in any form. At the same time the US imposed an economic blockade which closed off export markets for Nicaraguan goods.

There is no question who was responsible for the misery that the Nicaraguan people had to suffer, who was responsible for the re-introduction of hunger, for the raising of infant mortality, for the increasing illiteracy. That responsibility lay with the United States. By these means, the US government calculated to make life so intolerable for the majority of Nicaraguans that they would reject the Sandinistas in order to survive.

Yet even this is not enough to explain why the people of Nicaragua voted in February 1990 to accept the UNO coalition, so clearly linked with the murderous Contras, and reject the Sandinistas who had carried the banner of their own mass insurrection since 1979. Yes, there was misery. Yes, there was hunger. Yes, there was war-weariness. But the Nicaraguan people had accepted that sacrifice for ten years. They had fought, they had died, they had heroically sustained a struggle against imperialism under the worst of conditions. They had done so, and supported their own leaders—in the 1984 elections, for example, they gave an overwhelming majority of votes to the Sandinistas.

Why, in the six years between the elections of 1984 and those of 1990, did the electoral support of the Sandinistas change so catastrophically? To answer this question, we need to look not just at the external factors of war, poverty and US aggression, but at the Sandinistas' own policies—particularly in response to the aspirations of the mass movement whose banners they carried. What did they offer to the workers and peasants who had made the Nicaraguan revolution?

> For the Sandinistas, representative democracy, national elections and the existence of democratic organs of the state—as important as they are—must be subordinated to a concept of democracy that links state power to popular power, that guarantees, as Comandante Bayardo Arce has said, that the 'construction of the new society will be carried out under the leadership of the previously dominated classes'.[4]

What had brought about the apparent change of direction that gave priority not to building 'popular democracy', but to elections to a bourgeois parliament? What was this 'popular democracy' that the Sandinistas said they were building? Did it go 'beyond socialism', as they claimed? Why was the United States, a nation of 280 million people and immense economic power, so anxious to crush a movement in one of the world's poorest and weakest countries, a country of little power and little strategic significance?

This book sets out to answer these questions. The analysis it offers, though brought together in the weeks following the Sandinistas' election defeat, is not made with the benefit of hindsight. It has grown over the past eleven years, alongside the process that it seeks to understand: the road taken by Nicaragua after the mass overthrow of the dictator Somoza in July 1979.

Chapter two

Insurrection*

ON 16 July 1979, five people boarded a plane in Costa Rica; they were on their way to Leon, the second city of Nicaragua. The five constituted the Provisional Government of Reconstruction of Nicaragua. They represented different social forces. Daniel Ortega was a member of the National Directorate of the Frente Sandinista (FSLN); Moises Hassan, a mathematician, and Sergio Ramirez, a writer, were long-standing members of the Frente. The other two came from very different backgrounds. Alfonso Robelo, a wealthy cotton farmer and industrialist, was leader of the National Democratic Movement (MDN) and head of the private enterprise organisation COSEP; Violeta Chamorro was the widow of a newspaper editor who had led the bourgeois opposition to Somoza for many years.

As the plane landed, Anastasio Somoza, the last of a dynasty that had determined the destiny of Nicaragua since 1934, was in his concrete bunker, built on a hill at the centre of the capital, Managua, overlooking the lake of Tiscapa. From there he was directing a massive military operation throughout the city. During the day, planes bombed factories and hospitals, while helicopters dropped 500lb oildrums full of explosive on the working-class districts. Later, the National Guard, a highly trained military force that was the basis of his power, swept through the same districts, killing and torturing—partly in search of hidden members of the Frente Sandinista, partly in order to terrorise the population.

---

* Chapters 2, 3 and 4 first appeared as part of an article, 'The Nicaraguan Revolution', in **International Socialism** 2:17 (autumn 1982) and were re-published in the book **Nicaragua: Revolution under siege** (Bookmarks 1985).

That night in the bunker, and surrounded by the elite of the National Guard, Somoza and his mistress Dinorah Sampson drank too much and listened to the radio reports. What they heard was that six of Nicaragua's main towns were under the control of insurrectionary forces. Many of the National Guard had either succumbed to the people's vengeance or were being held for trial. The streets were controlled by young men and women wearing the red and black of the Sandinistas and carrying every kind of weapon, from sophisticated automatics to machetes.

The next day, 17 July, Somoza fled the country, on his way to Miami. He had destroyed almost everything he could not take with him; like those in his immediate circle, he had been sending money out of the country for years. Before he left, Somoza passed the presidency to the Congressional leader, Urcuyo, whose job was to hand over power, formally, to the provisional government. But Urcuyo announced, unexpectedly, that he intended to remain in power until the scheduled 1981 elections.

The announcement killed the last attempts by the US government to exercise some control over the manner of Somoza's downfall. It was now the Frente Sandinista, undisputed leader of the armed rising, which seized the initiative—and the insurrectionaries began their march on the capital. By the afternoon of 19 July, all vestiges of the former state had gone.

*   *   *

Only six months earlier, the Nicaraguan bourgeoisie had believed it was in control of the situation. Mass risings in Matagalpa, Leon and Esteli in September 1978 had been followed by massive 'Clean-Up' operations by the National Guard which left 6,000 dead. The bourgeois political organisations, grouped in a broad opposition front, the FAO, assumed that this signalled defeat for the insurrectionary strategy of the FSLN, and turned to the United States for a negotiated solution. A Mediation Commission was set up to organise Somoza's resignation and ensure an 'orderly transfer of power'. Had Somoza resigned promptly, things later might have been very different—but he refused to give up his power. From that moment on, a negotiated solution was no longer possible.

For its part the FSLN retreated to the hills with large numbers of new recruits. It was short of arms—but far from crushed.

In November, the FSLN walked out of the opposition front, taking with it the trade unions and the Nicaraguan Communist Party (the PSN). In February the following year, 1979, these organisations formed the Revolutionary Patriotic Front under FSLN leadership. In the same month, the US stopped arms sales to Somoza; two months later, Mexico broke off diplomatic relations.

In March, the final offensive began in Esteli. 'The FSLN's tactic was to create an indefinite number of operational zones through combinations of strike movements, local uprisings and the activity of its own military units.'[1] In military terms, this was designed to disperse the forces of the National Guard; politically, it represented a co-ordination of the three areas of FSLN activity, each of which had been developed by a different tendency.

The conditions were right. Several thousand combatants moved in from the war fronts, better armed than before. In the cities, the mass movement was also preparing for a final thrust —and the bombing of Esteli did nothing to hold back the preparations.

On 4 June, the Sandinistas issued a call for an insurrectional general strike. The next day, everything stopped; and the cities prepared for the final confrontation with the Guard. On 10 June, Managua rose in battle—it was spontaneous and occurred earlier than planned. By the end of the month it was clear that, until the rest of the country was consolidated in the hands of the insurrection, Managua could not hold out against the savage assault of the Guard. The FSLN determined a strategic withdrawal, and 6,000 people (or more) marched through the night the 25 kilometres to Masaya. The vengeance wreaked by Somoza in Managua was terrible; yet Masaya was almost impregnable. Fourteen days later, the final assault on Managua brought the Somoza regime to its end.

The final weeks had been extraordinarily bloody. The Guard had embarked on an orgy of revenge and murder; yet this only swelled the ranks of the insurrection. There was now no turning back. The young, the very young, the old were all involved. The barricades made out of Somoza's paving stones rose up throughout the city. The contact bombs and home-made weapons would have to be enough—there was nothing left to lose.

By early July, the United States—which had played the usual

dual role, cutting arms but voting for emergency aid for Somoza—instructed its Managua ambassador, Lawrence Pezzullo, to stay in his hotel and not present his credentials to Somoza. Meanwhile, its Central American representative, William Bowdler, was in Costa Rica, trying for the last time to ensure a National Guard presence in the provisional government. But no one was speaking to Somoza.

In the end the diplomatic manoeuvres and political discussions had little effect on what happened on those July days. In the eight weeks after Jinotega was taken, it was the masses in insurrection who seized command. It was the people themselves who, step by step, took back the streets.

The Somoza state was now overthrown. The 'orderly transfer of power', which the bourgeoisie argued for, did not occur. Instead, the FSLN seized state power at the head of a mass insurrectionary movement. As the columns of fighters entered Managua throughout the day, they had behind them an armed people, the embryo of a new army to replace the National Guard—which was the force on which Somoza's power had always rested, and whose final destruction guaranteed his downfall.

The basis of a new form of social organisation had been glimpsed in the course of the insurrection; in the Civil Defence Committees, the Popular Militias and the Sandinista Agricultural Communes.

The hegemony of the FSLN in this new Nicaragua was undisputed. The revolution in a narrow sense—the armed overthrow of the state and the abolition of its armed force by popular insurrection—had taken place. The revolution in a broad sense, however—the assumption of power over the whole of society by the working class—faced a series of limitations which derived from the peculiar character of Nicaragua's historical development. It would be impossible to explain Sandinismo, or the circumstances in which it came to power, without understanding that history.

Chapter three

The rise of the Somoza dictatorship

THE economic structure of Nicaragua was to a large extent determined by the end of the last century. Until the 1890s, economic activity was divided between the great cattle ranches of the ruling families and small communities engaged in the subsistence production of maize and beans. Coffee was first planted in 1850, but from 1890 onwards its rising price on the world market accelerated production. As more land was devoted to the new crop, communal lands were absorbed into the plantations. The peasant population remained as seasonal labour or was driven further into the interior in search of land. The fierce resistance of the indigenous population was crushed.[1] This pattern of dispossession and proletarianisation—the creation of a working class whose only means of survival was to work for wages —continued as export agriculture developed, creating a growing seasonal labour force, some of whom were able (barely) to survive for the rest of the year from the produce of their tiny isolated plots of land.[2]

With expanding coffee production, a new bourgeoisie emerged, opposed to the old ruling families and linked to the world market. Its political philosophy—liberalism—and its advocacy of centralisation, national integration and free trade reflected its aims: to centralise control over national resources in support of the expanding new industry, and to increase profits by diversifying markets and sources of capital and manufactures. This was the programme of Zelaya, who was in power between 1893 and 1909. Zelaya succeeded in establishing central control over the national economy and tying it to coffee, and in creating a 'free' labour force through dispossession.

At the same time, Zelaya established relations with European capital. It was this which most sorely provoked the imperialist power to the north—the United States. In the first place, US capital (then in its most aggressive 'dollar diplomacy' phase) was unhappy about losing a key area of investment in Central America. Secondly, Nicaragua had then—before the construction of the Panama Canal—been singled out as the location for the strategic canal between Atlantic and Pacific oceans. When Zelaya offered the canal contract to a consortium of European companies, US capital rose in protest, and found a sympathetic ear in secretary of state Philander Knox, who happened to be a director of a company with interests on Nicaragua's Atlantic coast.

Zelaya's government was overthrown in 1909. American marines landed at Bluefields, on the Atlantic coast, and assumed direct control. By the time the Bryan-Chamorro Pact was signed in 1912, the US had established complete control over Nicaragua, not only appointing presidents, but also imposing a plan for economic 'stabilisation' to be overseen by a mixed US-Nicaraguan Commission. The real meaning of the plan emerged clearly when, in exchange for a short-term loan of $100,000, American banks assumed direct control of the Nicaraguan Customs, the railways, the National Bank and the collection of taxes.[3] Zelaya's plan for the development of an autonomous national state, capable of renegotiating the terms of its unequal insertion into the world economy, lay in ruins.

Between 1909 and 1926, the liberal bourgeoisie supported a number of armed risings against the regime, bids for power where no electoral means existed. Their banners were nationalism and development; but the weakness of the bourgeoisie, its incapacity to accumulate, ensured that the slogan of national development was never more than words:

> The role that might have corresponded to the incipient national industry, was occupied at a very early stage by external suppliers, thus deepening the subordination of the Nicaraguan economy in its relations with the centres that had hegemony over world trade.[4]

The last great liberal rising under Moncada in 1926 proved to be just another bid for a share of power, and ended in an agreement between liberals, conservatives and the US which took

Moncada to the presidency. This time, however, there was a difference. One of the liberal generals, Augusto Cesar Sandino, refused to lay down his arms. For the next seven years, he led a struggle against US intervention that again took up the call for independent national development, though this time in a more radical form, and carried much further the battle against imperialism.

Sandino, born in the village of Niquinohomo in 1895, was vilified and dismissed as a bandit and madman for forty years after his death. Yet in the countryside he was remembered; after 1979 it was his name, and the outline of his famous stetson hat, that graced almost every wall in Nicaragua. Sandino's 'crazy little army' was often reduced, in the course of its struggle, to a handful of starving people; yet he was known in the rest of the world, and his portrait hung behind the platform at the Brussels Anti-Imperialist Congress of 1928.[5]

Sandino's was a peasant army, though his own ideas were framed by liberalism:

> We must expel completely from our homeland all North American citizens and capital, who represent an imminent danger for the nation that innocently received them into its midst. We must develop our own industry and our own trade... Our project is based on the right of peoples to express their opinion... on the liberty and independence of our republics... and on the wonderful natural privileges with which God has endowed these countries and which have been the cause of the domination exercised over us.[6]

Sandino's 1927 Political Manifesto assigns the struggle to the oppressed; its political perspective is nationalist, its economic idea rooted in national development.[7] It was in no sense an anti-capitalist programme (Sandino wanted a consortium of Latin American capital to take charge of the canal project), and its politics seem to be derived mainly from the petit-bourgeois anti-imperialism of the Peruvian APRA party. The programme identified imperialism as the main obstacle to development, and foresaw a new form of agriculture-based development, organised through a cooperative community of small landowners, self-sufficient in food, and growing towards a healthy, Latin American agrarian capitalism. There is nothing in Sandino's writings to suggest a vision of industrial growth, though in this he did no more than reflect the reality of a Nicaragua with no industrial sector outside the isolated US-owned mines, no industrial proletariat except the semi-enslaved Indian miners and lumber workers in the US enclaves of the Atlantic coast,[8] and a stagnant agro-export economy serviced by a semi-proletarian labour force.

It was the undiversified nature of that economy that explained why the world recession at the end of the 1920s hit Nicaragua early and hard. Its victims swelled Sandino's army. In the 1920s, 90 per cent of the population were hungry, 50 per cent of Nicaragua's children died before they were nine, and 75 per cent of the people had no education at all.[9]

As the struggle developed, and Sandino understood that 'only the workers and the peasants will take the struggle through to its ultimate consequences', Sandino's manifestos began to move towards an alternative form of socio-economic organisation—the aim was to set up peasant cooperatives within a liberated area, such as the community of Wiwili, formed in the course of the war.

The radicalisation of the military struggle, the shift from regular to guerrilla warfare, took Sandino closer to a concept of 'people's war' based on the peasantry. The new tactic was in part dictated by the conduct of the war itself; the US Marines took savage measures of reprisal against Sandino's base of support—including air raids on the town of Ocotal in 1927,[10] terror, the selective murder of civilians and the removal of whole communities to 'strategic hamlets'. As a military tactician, Sandino was very able; his conduct of the war, after the first costly attempts at trench warfare, turned on an extremely mobile form of guerrilla war based on ambush and escape—a tactic which assumed a close identification between guerrilla army and peasants, and guaranteed an intimate knowledge of the terrain and the ability of the guerrillas to fade back into the rural population.

At the political level, Sandino's vision was limited by the objective reality. His irritable dismissal of Farabundo Marti, once his secretary and later leader of the Communist Party of El Salvador and organiser of the 1932 peasant insurrection there, suggested Sandino's resistance to socialist politics.[11] Yet in practice he also understood that the servile bourgeoisie of

Nicaragua was too weak to carry forward the project of national liberation and that the social force for achieving this programme would have the peasantry at its core—they alone would do the fighting.

Humberto Ortega has argued that Sandino's movement was class-based, and that it had working-class demands.[12] While the class composition of the guerrilla army was clear, the alliance that was its political basis centred on the expulsion of the Americans. When that was achieved (on 1 February 1933), Sandino's petit-bourgeois support disappeared, and Sandino himself withdrew to Wiwili, taking a small military force with him to protect the community. Ortega describes this withdrawal as being rather like Mao's Long March—as a tactic of accumulation of forces. There is nothing in Sandino's writings to suggest this—in any event, we shall never know. A year later, the hired thugs of the first Anastasio Somoza, who was now head of the National Guard, murdered Sandino in the street. In the next two days, Wiwili was destroyed and its inhabitants shot to pieces.

With Sandino's death, the project for national development remained untried. And a weak bourgeoisie finally preferred a consolidation of the agro-export model under Somoza to the structural changes Sandino had argued for.

Anastasio Somoza made his first profits from forging dollar bills and selling used cars in the United States. His knowledge of English got him a job as interpreter for the occupying US Marines in Nicaragua. By 1933, the US commander had named him head of the National Guard—and it was this control over the armed force of the state that enabled him to seize power after the US withdrawal and found a dynasty that would last for more than forty years.

Somoza's role was to consolidate the agro-export model of the Nicaraguan economy. As coffee prices fell, the landowners simply annexed more land and raised the quantity produced. The production of subsistence crops suffered as more peasants were dispossessed,[13] but Somoza's strong state was there to stifle any resistance to the process. He exacted a high price for his trouble; the bourgeoisie was obliged to pay new taxes direct to Somoza, state employees had to make a 5 per cent contribution from their salary to finance Somoza's new political party, and foreign companies paid direct tributes in exchange for the right to operate in their Atlantic coast enclaves without interference. These contributions, together with German property expropriated during the Second World War, converted Somoza into the biggest private landowner in Nicaragua. By 1944, he owned 51 cattle ranches, 46 coffee estates and eight sugar plantations, as well as a personal fortune of over $60 million—the fruit of wartime profiteering.[14]

The interrelationship with the US economy had deepened during the war, as Nicaragua became almost exclusively a supplier of raw materials for the US. But the period brought protests from the bourgeoisie, which felt it was paying too dearly for Somoza's protection. In 1944, the announcement that Somoza would be standing for election again in 1947 provoked mass student protests and the formation of the Independent Liberal Party (PLI).[15]

In the same year the Nicaraguan Communist Party, the PSN, was formed—at a meeting in support of Somoza.[16] And the same year had seen strikes among rubber workers, and by bus drivers and textile workers in Leon and Managua.[17] If the PSN ever had ambitions to build on working-class activity, Somoza swept the ground from under their feet. On 1 May 1945, a new Labour Code was passed, guaranteeing wages, social services and so on. Somoza's price for this was social peace, and it was a price the PSN accepted on the basis of the USSR's call for the formation of broad anti-fascist alliances, a policy which had already led to the voluntary dissolution of some Communist Parties and the inclusion of others in bourgeois governments (as in Cuba). When the 'anti-fascist' Somoza turned against his erstwhile ally, the PSN could offer no resistance to the repression unleashed after 1947. The Labour Code, of course, was never implemented.

By 1950, the bourgeoisie was reconciled with Somoza. A new period of agro-export expansion began, based principally on the growth in cotton production (from 379 tons exported in 1949 to 43,791 in 1955; by 1960, cotton represented 23 per cent of total exports).[18] For the bourgeoisie, the first consideration was a harmonious process of expansion—even though this meant a recognition that the Somoza state was an essential component of their relationship with imperialism and the world market.[19]

In this period, opposition was limited to the tiny Independent Liberal Party, whose youth section was a crucible for many of those who would later form the Frente Sandinista. It produced, too, the student-poet Rigoberto Lopez Perez, who in 1956 assassinated Somoza at a banquet. In the months of repression that followed, it became clear that it was not to be the 'beginning of the end' that Rigoberto had predicted; for Somoza's two sons, Luis (who became president in 1957) and Anastasio (who had followed his father as head of the National Guard) were well-trained to maintain the dynasty.[20]

Under Luis Somoza, the repression of the rural population continued, but there was a relative liberalisation in the urban areas—permitted by the general agreement which had been reached between Somoza and the bourgeoisie after 1950. The pact was based on a clear definition of territories, of zones of operation. Thus Luis Somoza could become a pillar of the gradualist, developmentalist strategies represented by the Alliance for Progress, which was set up by the United States after 1959 to isolate the Cuban Revolution and form a solid military and political alliance to maintain that isolation. (The Bay of Pigs invasion of Cuba in 1961, for example, was launched from Nicaragua.) As part of the same 'reformist' policy, Luis Somoza even ceded power to a civilian, René Schick, between 1963 and 1967. Under Schick, the level of political opposition rose, and union organisation, although tiny, drew in increasing numbers as industry expanded under the impact of the Central American Common Market. Direct US investment increased,[21] the infrastructure was expanded[22] and urban assembly and consumer industries developed. The financial bourgeoisie greatly extended its operations, forming two powerful new financial-industrial groups—BANIC and BANAMERICA[23]—with the tacit approval of Somoza. Yet in the countryside, social relations were characterised by poverty, dispossession, hunger and deepening exploitation. This was the model of 'reform with repression', of a deepening contradiction between country and city. The model lasted until 1967.

As its economic power grew, the conservative opposition again prepared a challenge for political power, based on an active student movement and a growing trade union organisation, linked through the first bourgeois political front, the ONU. Its bid for control of the state ended in the mass demonstration of 22 January 1967, which was brutally repressed, leaving 400 dead. The demonstration marked a new phase, as Anastasio Somoza assumed direct control after the death of his brother. Once again, the bourgeoisie entered a pact with the dynasty. For the next five years, the Somozas embarked on a new period of accumulation —but they shared its fruits with what Jaime Wheelock calls this 'consular bourgeoisie', which had fought only for power *within* the structure, but had never challenged the structure itself.

By the end of the 1960s, US investors began to withdraw from Central America and turn their capital towards armaments or to investments in the developed world.[24] Throughout Latin America, the contradiction at the heart of the Alliance for Progress was beginning to be revealed.[25] Anastasio Somoza II himself directed his investments into new fields; he turned to the 'sunbelt' financiers, such as Howard Hughes and Robert Vesco, and to the Cuban exiles of Miami, for joint ventures into the more immediately rewarding fields of construction, gambling, drugs and prostitution.

On 29 December 1972, the centre of Managua was destroyed by a huge earthquake. Between 10,000 and 20,000 people died in the ruins, and 75 per cent of housing and 90 per cent of commerce were destroyed. The United Nations estimated the damage at $772 million. An international appeal was launched, and this aid provided the basis for the third and most speculative period of Somocista accumulation. The aid was earmarked for immediate relief and reconstruction. The centre of Managua ten years later, with its gaping torn buildings and vast empty spaces still lumpy with rubble, was eloquent testimony to the mockery Somoza made of the relief programme. While most of Managua's shops were destroyed, members of the National Guard set up makeshift stalls in the streets selling the medicines, clothes and food sent by international organisations. The cash aid was appropriated by Somoza himself and invested in a series of speculative projects—mainly construction. It was not public housing he built, of course, but shopping centres and middle-class residential areas, or new roads surfaced with the curious hexagonal road tiles made exclusively in one of Somoza's factories. For the National Guard, who were the basis of Somoza's power and whose loyalty was maintained by a mix of corruption and internal terror,[26] the earthquake provided an unparalleled opportunity for pillage and profit. For a week or so, 600 American troops maintained 'law and order', while the Guard ransacked Managua.

The two years that followed were a period of economic boom, fuelled by the construction industry. They were also years of drought, bringing hunger to the rural population and drawing waves of migrants to the slum *barrios*, the poor working-class districts of Managua. Trade union activity was unprecedented; in 1973, building workers launched a major strike for a 10 per cent wage rise and against Somoza's attempt to lengthen the working week from 48 to 60 hours. Strikes by workers in health and the textile industry followed. The bourgeoisie, too, took to the streets in protest against Somoza's monopolisation of the post-earthquake bonanza.

Despite this 'false boom', the 1970s were a period of economic recession. This intensified the struggle between Somoza and a bourgeoisie who saw the shrinking product of the agro-export economy being increasingly redistributed towards Somoza. Yet the bourgeoisie had no political alternative to offer; as the bourgeois opposition grew, and formed its new broad front organisation, UDEL, its perspectives remained fundamentally electoral. The political agitation and open criticism of Somoza, however, were taken up by other sectors. The three trade union federations, as well as the PSN, joined the broad opposition front.

The rural workers, the peasants and the urban poor—whose conditions of life were deteriorating rapidly—had no political expression; yet it was they who had known the full force of Somoza's repression—the arbitrary dispossession by landowners with the support of the Guard, extortion by the network of spies and informers set up by Somoza, arbitrary arrests and torture in the urban *barrios*. It was their bitterness and anger that was to explode in February 1978. These were the sectors of the population that the FSLN saw as the motor of the armed struggle against Somocismo.

Chapter four

Growth of the Sandinista resistance

SANDINO'S MURDER in 1934 brought the possibility of resistance to an effective end, though some of his aides, such as Pedro Altamirano, tried to sustain the struggle for a short time. The renewed mass activity of 1944-47 proved short-lived, as the reimposition of the state of siege in 1947 closed all doors to open political opposition. A frustrated conservative opposition turned to arms not in an attempt to develop the armed struggle as such, but rather in an attempt to identify dissident elements within the National Guard and challenge Somoza from within. It was the classic model of the 'palace coup'.[1] Repression also followed the assassination of the first Somoza in 1956. Among those arrested and tortured was Pedro Joaquin Chamorro, later editor of *La Prensa*.[2]

The economic crisis of the late 1950s provided the conditions for renewed mass activity.[3] To worsening conditions in the countryside were added new confrontations in the cities. The number of trade unions rose from five to eighteen in 1958 alone, and the student movement, influenced by the Cuban revolution, became increasingly active. Yet the movement had no unified political direction. The Conservative Party had once again reached an agreement with Somoza; and the Independent Liberal Party, though it produced many of the student leaders, was unable to provide the necessary leadership.

Nor was there any revolutionary organisation capable of filling the vacuum.[4] There had been virtually no urban working class in Nicaragua until the late 1950s, and the PSN had been content to build a narrow base among the small groups of workers that did exist, and to ignore the agricultural proletariat.

Furthermore, the PSN's early compromises with Somoza, and its determination to operate within a legal framework, left it wide open to repression on the one hand, and gained it a collaborationist reputation on the other. Socialist politics, therefore, were to an extent discredited; the vacuum was filled by a mixture of liberalism and vague references to Sandino. In 1956, a small group of students started a Marxist study circle at the University of Leon—but it was to the Cuban interpretation of revolutionary practice that they turned.

The Frente de Liberacion Nacional itself was founded in Honduras, in 1961, by Carlos Fonseca, Tomas Borge and Silvio Mayorga. Its roots were in the student movement, and its theory came from Cuba.[5] In 1963, the word Sandinista was added—and the organisation became the Frente Sandinista, the FSLN. It was more than a change of name: Fonseca had argued from the outset for a politics derived from Sandino—guerrilla war based on the peasantry.[6] In this context, mass work meant preparation of a support network for the armed revolutionaries, and a strong rejection of the kind of public activity—demonstrations, public protests—that were identified with the PSN. For a short time, Fonseca and the others had held out some hope that the line of the PSN could be changed—the formation of the FSLN buried that idea.

The FSLN's first guerrilla action, at Rio Coco and Bocay in 1963, proved a costly failure. Its defeat coincided with a period of liberalisation under Schick which seemed, albeit briefly, to vindicate the PSN policy of operating within legal limits. As Fonseca put it:

> We hesitated about presenting a clear Marxist-Leninist ideology ... the result, in part, of the attitude of the traditional Marxist-Leninist sector in the popular struggle which, in practice, had openly participated in the manoeuvres of the Somocista clique.[7]

For the next two years, the FSLN worked in the student movement and through a broad electoral organisation called Republican Mobilisation. The strategy of 'accumulating forces for the guerrilla' was put into abeyance. In the countryside, the Sandinista organiser Rigoberto Cruz did important work in forming some of the first peasant organisations. Many of the new cadres of the FSLN came from these two sectors.

Fonseca, meanwhile, was in Cuba. He returned in 1966, convinced of the correctness of a guerrilla strategy, and began to prepare a new *foco*—a guerrilla base—in Pancasan. At the same time, the period of liberalisation ended with the killing of 400 people on the mass demonstration of 22 January 1967. By August, the Pancasan guerrilla group, too, was destroyed. It was true that the group had included a number of peasants, and that the FSLN had drawn new recruits from its mass work in the previous three years. Yet it was equally true that mass work was still seen to imply the mobilisation of peasant *support*, rather than its direct organised participation in the guerrilla struggle. The revolutionaries, not the masses, were regarded as the subjects of history. And the next *foco*, at Zinica in 1969, was founded on the same basis. Henry Ruiz, known as 'Modesto', summed up these attitudes later when he said: 'A worker who is transferred to the mountains becomes a far greater danger to the Somocista regime than an economic strike carried out by hundreds of workers'.[8]

At the beginning of the 1970s the FSLN was therefore still a tiny organisation. It had little or no role in the series of workers' struggles of 1970-74. Its strategy at the time was again the 'silent accumulation of forces', which again took it into the cities in search of new members. It now worked in a clandestine way. The strategy had several pivots. First, the FSLN was active (though not overtly) in the student mobilisations of the period, directing them towards campaigns for the release of Sandinista political prisoners, many of whom were suffering terrible tortures in Somoza's jails.[9] Secondly, there was peasant work, in its turn conducted under the cover of the activities of the liberation church, which had begun to move in the direction of radical social action after the Medellin Conference. The majority of the FSLN National Directorate of the 1980s, for example, came into politics through radical Christian groups.[10]

The general leadership of the movement at this time was in the hands of the bourgeois opposition—though the building strike was led by the PSN. Clearly, if the FSLN was to justify its claim to the political leadership of the mass movement, it would have to respond. So, on 27 December 1974, the FSLN invaded the house of a prominent Somoza supporter, Chema Castillo, during a Christmas party, and held the guests under arms. The result of the action was the freeing of 18 Sandinista prisoners, the broadcasting of two FSLN communiques, half a million dollars and safe passage for the prisoners and their captors.[11]

There followed 33 months of savage repression of the peasantry, and the unrelenting persecution of the FSLN in both the city and the mountains, as Somoza declared a state of siege. The FSLN was thus unable to follow up or build upon the Christmas raid.

The debate in the FSLN

At this point a fierce debate arose within the FSLN. The theory that gave priority to the building of guerrilla bases in the countryside (based on Che Guevara's book **Guerrilla Warfare**) had been abandoned after Zinica, and the argument was between the advocates of a strategy of people's war, based on a slow preparation of the rural population for prolonged war (the GPP group), and a 'Proletarian' Tendency (TP), which argued that the central task was to organise among the working class, in both country and city, and to build a revolutionary party. While the GPP still identified with the Sandinista orthodoxy defined by Carlos Fonseca, the Proletarian Tendency laid stress on the growth of the working class through the 1960s and 1970s, and on its increasing combativity. Jaime Wheelock, one of the Proletarian Tendency leaders, pointed out in his book *Imperialismo v dictadura* that despite the predominance of Somoza, there did exist a clearly defined bourgeoisie in Nicaragua. Thus Sandinismo should be extended, and a clear perception of anti-capitalist, class struggle added to its anti-imperialist content.

The internal rift was a bitter one, and was aggravated by the difficulties of communication between the two groups. When Fonseca returned to Nicaragua in 1976, it was in order to maintain a dialogue; his death in action soon afterwards made the split deeper.

For the next year and a half the groups worked in virtual isolation from one another. Yet there seemed to be a basic agreement that the overthrow of Somoza would require a long period of preparation and organisation—and that when the revolution did occur, it would mark the beginning of a transition to socialism.[13] In 1976, however, a third tendency emerged—the

Terceristas, or Insurrectionists. They argued that an alliance built on a more limited anti-Somocista base could bring about the fall of Somoza sooner than expected. The formation of such an alliance, both nationally and internationally, combined with spectacular commando-type actions, would—they believed—precipitate the crisis of Somocismo.

Though it is hard to describe people engaged in armed struggle as social-democrats, as Henri Weber points out, the Terceristas were fundamentally concerned with exploiting divisions within the bourgeoisie (particularly in view of the changing line of the US government). The complement to this would be a mass strike or insurrection, rather than long-term organisational work. In this sense, they could be described as Castroist.[14] By mid-1977, the Terceristas had clearly captured the leadership of the FSLN.

The Terceristas undoubtedly set aside the question of organising workers and peasants for their own liberation—which the GPP and the Proletarian Tendency had at least put on the agenda. Yet none of the three tendencies discussed the question of socialism, or saw the relationship between the construction of a revolutionary party rooted in the working class and the nature of state power after a revolutionary overthrow of the Somoza state. The transition to socialism was mentioned in the documents —but the role of the working class as the protagonist of that transition was not specifically discussed. There was no concept of workers' power, no sense of what a workers' state would be like, no preparation of a material base for such a state (by making support for the workers' own struggles a priority). In part, the lack of such discussion was the fruit of the particular history of the FSLN, of its emergence and growth outside the working-class movement, tiny though it was.

The result was that, when the mass upsurge of 1978 did occur, and when the overthrow of Somoza followed in July 1979, there was no political current present within the FSLN arguing for workers' power, for the struggle for socialism, or for the centrality of the working class in that process. The unification of the three FSLN tendencies in March 1979 represented, in one sense, the pressure of the mass upsurge on the FSLN; on the other hand, it also reflected the failure to develop an alternative leadership informed with class politics. It is in this sense that the question of the revolutionary party—the expression of that alternative leadership—becomes critically important, and its absence from internal political debate within the FSLN was a key element in post-revolutionary developments.

They were right, nevertheless, to argue that the situation was explosive. Between 1960 and 1977, the rural population had fallen from 60 per cent to 40 per cent of the total. Those who had left the countryside were mainly resident in the urban slums, devoid of even the most elementary welfare provision. By 1977, while 5 per cent of the population enjoyed an average income of $5,409 per head,[15] the majority of the people had an average annual income of $286. The period after the false boom of 1972-74 was marked by factory closures, massive lay-offs and rising unemployment. Sixty per cent of the rural population was literally hungry, and 70 per cent illiterate. Yet in 1978, Somoza closed the schools in order to save money for the purchase of arms!

By September 1977, the human rights policy pursued by US president Jimmy Carter led to the suspension of arms sales after the US Senate had heard the report of Fernando Cardenal, a Jesuit priest, on the appalling human rights situation in Nicaragua.[16] In response, Somoza lifted the state of siege in October—and an explosion of popular protest immediately followed. The October mobilisations were led by the broad opposition front, which saw them as a form of pressure designed to force the US to intervene and depose Somoza.

At the same time, however, the Terceristas launched a series of attacks on National Guard barracks at San Carlos, Ocotal and Masaya. While not particularly successful—they generated no immediate mass response—they did establish the military capacity of the FSLN. At the political level, the Terceristas had brought together a number of influential supporters in the Group of Twelve (a group of businessmen, intellectuals and priests supporting the FSLN), who followed up the military actions with a political declaration arguing that the FSLN was now a political force that could not be excluded from any political solution to the crisis of Somocismo. The FSLN undoubtedly enjoyed a moral authority based on its long and heroic history of struggle; yet it was still unconnected with an organised mass base.

Civil War

In January 1978, the situation changed dramatically. Pedro Joaquin Chamorro, editor of **La Prensa** and leader of the opposition front, was murdered by Somoza. 120,000 people marched at his funeral, and the opposition front called a national 'bosses' strike' for 23 January. The political objective was still an orderly removal of Somoza with US backing.

But at the beginning of February the bourgeoisie lost the power to stem the flow of events. The initiative passed to the community of Monimbo, on the outskirts of the city of Masaya, where there was an explosion of accumulated anger and resentment against a repressive state. For a week the local people held off a full-scale National Guard assault. And though the Proletarian Tendency of the FSLN was working in the area, the leadership of the rising was exclusively local.[17]

Although the Monimbo rising was finally crushed, and a terrible vengeance wreaked by Somoza, it was clear that it had detonated what would be the definitive military confrontation in the urban *barrios*. The Terceristas, who lost one of their main leaders in the battle, dissolved their rural cadres into the cities; the GPP moved its bases closer to the populated areas, and the Proletarian Tendency turned to the military and political organisation of the urban masses. Despite the repression, the mass movement was now growing at all levels. The Agricultural Workers Union was formed by Sandinista peasants in early 1978, and the Civil Defence Committees emerged as new forms of mass self-organisation in the war zone. While the FSLN did not lead or organise all these movements, it was their slogans that appeared on the walls.

From now on, mass activity hardly abated. When the Group of Twelve returned to Managua in July 1978 in defiance of Somoza's prohibition, they were greeted by mass demonstrations. Their return was timed to coincide with the formation of a new bourgeois front, the FAO, led by cotton farmer and industrialist Alfonso Robelo. The Group of Twelve were not initially part of the FAO—they entered it on their arrival in Managua, but only with the intention of taking over its leadership or splitting it.

The insurrections of September 1978 further enhanced the

authority of the FSLN. They began in August, in Matagalpa, in the wake of the spectacular assault on the National Palace on 28 August,[18] when the FSLN had kidnapped the entire Congress and released them only in exchange for 59 Sandinista prisoners and the publication of two political statements. Yet the Matagalpa rising was not led by the FSLN—it was fundamentally spontaneous. As the risings spread, the FSLN had no choice but to assume the leadership[19]—or lose the opportunity forever. Though it was ill-prepared for an armed struggle on that scale, the FSLN did take the leadership of the risings in Leon and Esteli, which followed that in Matagalpa. When the risings ended, the FSLN withdrew into the mountains, with its authority reinforced and its ranks swollen with new recruits from among the street fighters.

The Guard moved in, arresting anyone who could have handled a weapon, and everyone whose youth made them potential recruits for the FSLN. The violence was terrible, yet it did not seem to daunt a population that had already known so much brutality and death. The FAO opposition front, however, interpreted the moment as the end of mass activity, and confidently launched a new initiative calling for US mediation. Talks continued until January 1979. The FSLN refused to participate in any form of 'Somocismo without Somoza', and in January Somoza himself broke off all further negotiations.

It was now clear that victory would mean insurrection, the overthrow of the Somoza state, and the abolition of the National Guard. That was the demand coming from a mass movement that could see the cracks appearing in the edifice of the state and the prospects of its own power. And the FSLN was the only political organisation capable of interpreting and directing that demand. In November the Group of Twelve walked out of the opposition front, together with the trade unions and the PSN; all then joined the FSLN-led United People's Movement. In February, this became the Popular Revolutionary Front under clear Sandinista leadership, and its open aim was to take power. The new alliance was broad in its social character, but united around its opposition to Somoza. Somoza's refusal to yield his own power in order to save the state had set the terms for the next and final phase of the struggle.

Only the FSLN was committed to the armed overthrow of

Somoza. The unification of its three tendencies enabled it to take military leadership of the mass movement, which was, in a confused way, posing the question of power. Yet, under Tercerista dominance, the FSLN channelled that feeling only towards the overthrow of Somoza. Beyond that, no section of the Sandinistas could offer a programme which looked to the assumption of power by that mass movement itself.

On 20 July 1979 the new, revolutionary Nicaragua was free of Somoza, who in one incarnation or another had dominated Nicaragua for 43 years. But the process of removing him had been costly. Four of Nicaragua's seven cities lay in ruins—Leon, Esteli, Matagalpa and Masaya, where only the twisted signs of the Masaya cinema remained amid the devastated streets surrounding the National Guard barracks.

Yet the atmosphere was exhilarating and euphoric. The urban *barrios* celebrated what they rightly saw as the exercise of their collective power,[20] tearing down with their bare hands the statue of Somoza outside the Somoza stadium which, in the words of the priest-poet Ernesto Cardenal,[21] had been put there precisely because it offended the people. The bourgeoisie, meanwhile, was trying the new revolutionary language for size...

Chapter five

The US dimension*

THE SOMOZAS, like the ruling families of other Central American states, had derived their power from their defence of the interests of the United States—both economic and political—inside Nicaragua and in the region. Their overthrow made US involvement inevitable. But what form would this take?

At first, the policy of US president Jimmy Carter seemed to favour the new regime. He had stopped arms sales to Somoza in February 1979 and, immediately after Somoza's overthrow, the US provided a limited amount of aid to the new government. Yet even that consisted of $70 million credit for the purchase of US foodstuffs, while only $5 million was given in direct aid, with the attached condition that it could not be used where Cuban or Russian personnel were employed. This meant that even that meagre sum could not be spent on health, education or teacher-training. To understand the link between this and the later massive aid given to the Contras and to UNO, we need to look at US imperial policies in the region.

The pattern of Nicaragua's development was influenced from the start by the proximity of US export markets. This was true of the whole region. Each of the economies of Central America had been dependent on export crops since their creation in the 1820s. In Nicaragua's case, this was first meat, then coffee. More and more land was taken over for the production of this profitable export, bringing the dispossession of indigenous communities, the eviction of small peasants from their lands and their virtual enslavement as labourers on the coffee plantations. The effect of

* Most of this chapter is taken from an article, 'Central America after the Arias Plan', in **International Socialism** 2:39 (summer 1988).

these changes was to concentrate land in the hands of a small coffee oligarchy, to which the state was entirely subordinate.

From the beginning of the century, therefore, the structure of Central American society reproduced the concentration of power and wealth among a tiny landed oligarchy linked to imperialism, at one end of the spectrum, and at the other the grinding poverty of a dispossessed rural population working on the great plantations for part of the year, while attempting to eke a living from the most inhospitable and remote lands where their tiny plots were located for the rest of the year. And for more and more of them, as the dynamic sector of the economy grew, even the prospect of a tiny parcel of land was lost. They became landless. It is that twin process of concentration and dispossession that marks the twentieth century experience of Central America.

The increasingly interventionist role of the United States was articulated in the restated Monroe Doctrine of the 1890s, in which (with familiar phrase and symbol) the US pronounced its God-given right[1] to assume control over the Central American area. In part, the US government was acting to legitimate and protect the interests of US capital seeking raw materials in Latin America, throwing its forces behind the competitive drive against the European capitals that had dominated the region in the nineteenth century—Britain on the Atlantic coast, France and Germany elsewhere.

Through the first decade of the century, the actions of the US state ensured the protection of the economic and territorial space into which US capital was expanding—Cuba 1898, Puerto Rico 1899, Panama 1903, Nicaragua 1908. These interventions established for the US a strategic bridgehead enabling it to control Atlantic-Pacific trade and ensure the secure movement of US capital through the region. While the US only sporadically exercised control directly, its interests and perspectives dominated and shaped the pattern of development and economic organisation throughout the region. By 1950, for example, the US accounted for 82 per cent of Central American exports, 75 per cent of imports and 90 per cent of foreign capital in the region.[2]

The history of Central America is in a way part of US history,[3] and its ruling classes have stoutly defended the advantages they have won from their faithful defence of US interests, against any and every attempt at reform. At times there have even been conflicts with the imperialists, but always temporary and always overridden by the global strategic concerns of imperialism.

Human rights, for example, have been an occasional matter for concern among liberal sectors of the American ruling class, especially when systematic abuses threatened to shift the balance of international support away from the US allies. But the general attitude is almost certainly closer to the views of the man who led the American Chamber of Commerce in Guatemala, Fred Sherwood, when in 1980 he reacted to complaints about human rights abuses by saying:

> Why should we be worried about the death squads? They're bumping off the commies, our enemies...[4]

Until the advent of Ronald Reagan, it was not customary for officials of the US administration to be quite as honest, but there was never any doubt about the criteria by which they judged their friends.

When president Jimmy Carter began in 1976 to speak of his concern for democracy and human rights, therefore, it should certainly have been treated with scepticism. Despite Carter's much-proclaimed religiosity, his 'new turn' had less to do with conscience than with a major shift in the balance of forces on a world scale. In 1973, the remnants of the American colonial power had left what was now called Ho Chi Minh City—Saigon was no more. There was no concealing the impact of that defeat.[5]

The authority of American power, consecrated at Yalta in 1944 as the Second World War reached its close and established on a series of battlefields from Greece to Korea in the years that followed, had reached its apotheosis in Vietnam. For 30 years, the discipline of the world economy had been assured by American military might. But now that discipline had been challenged, and the might of the world's most powerful capitalist policeman had proved incapable of destroying *politically* a small army of national liberation.

In the wake of its defeat in Vietnam, the US government had first and foremost to attend to its own disillusioned citizens, no longer sure of their national destiny to run the world. It had to re-establish the political consensus, and to regain its reputation as a mediator and a moderator in world affairs. This was not because of a change of heart—but because the US could not now send its troops wherever the system exhibited a tendency to fracture. If the re-establishment of US authority in the world could not be achieved by military means, then it must be achieved politically—that meant sweeping aside some of the military men and oligarchs who had faithfully served US interests in the past and replacing them with reformists capable of constructing the consensus.

Against that background, Carter's sudden advocacy of human rights was part of an attempt to strengthen the conservative reformists of the Latin American states against their old governors. But in Guatemala, El Salvador and Nicaragua, for example, the ruling groups had grown used to power and were not going to give it up easily. On the other side of the class divide, a rising level of mass mobilisation had already proved completely outside the control of any of the 'moderate' leaders. In such conditions, the US reluctance to continue to support its erstwhile allies only made them more resolute and more ruthless in defence of their power.

This was the climate in which the Nicaraguan revolution opened an unexpected new front in the Central American struggle. Two days before the revolutionary triumph, Urcuyo, appointed to oversee a caretaker regime after Somoza's departure, declared his intention to remain in power. He was swept aside by the mass movement. For the bourgeoisie was too weak simply to assume power. The coalition of forces organised in support of the Sandinistas—the Revolutionary Patriotic Front (FPR)—*could* occupy that role. When Carter finally stopped arms sales to Somoza in February 1979, after rising protests at home following the assassination of an ABC television reporter by Somoza's National Guard, the initiative lay with the FSLN.

The apparent acquiescence of the US administration towards the new revolutionary regime was because it was seen as an alliance of forces in which the bourgeoisie was not only represented, but had also salvaged some real influence. Carter's aim was 'the evolution of a pluralistic society with a mixed economy, not hostile to the United States'.[6] On the face of it, the assessment was correct, for the assumption was that Nicaragua's desperate need for external aid would make it impossible for the new government to sever the imperialist tie, and that such aid—coming mainly from the US and Western Europe—would carry implicit restraints on further radicalisation.

The temporary weakness of the United States had given the Sandinistas a breathing space. Their leadership of a mass movement that had toppled a seemingly impregnable dictator, a mass movement that carried all the hopes of the oppressed workers and peasants of Nicaragua, gave them an immense authority. Any revolutionary movement has political authority out of all proportion to the actual significance of the state it has conquered—as the impact of the Nicaraguan revolution on the oppressed workers and peasants of other Central American states was about to show.

The echoes of Nicaragua were heard throughout Latin America. In 1973, the government of Salvador Allende in Chile, which had inspired great hopes among the left, had fallen in a bloody military coup. In Latin America and beyond, that defeat provoked many on the reformist and Communist left to reconsider the possibilities for change. Their bleak conclusions became enshrined in the concept of the 'historic compromise' with social democracy, announced first by Enrico Berlinguer, general secretary of the Italian Communist Party, in the assessment of the events in Chile which he gave in November 1973. It amounted to a statement that revolution was now impossible.

The Nicaraguan revolution gave the lie to this. It offered hope to many of those on the left throughout the world who had been demoralised and disheartened by the defeat in Chile, or who could not rid themselves of the effects of the dead hand of Stalinism.

The Sandinistas, therefore, carried a great responsibility —but they had also been offered a tremendous opportunity. What would they make of it?

Chapter six

Strategy for a new society?*

THE economic inheritance left by Somoza was a grim bequest. Only $3.5 million was left in the National Bank; production in agriculture had fallen by more than 25 per cent (and much more in the food sector) and industrial activity had virtually ceased through June and July. What factories Somoza had not bombed were empty of stocks and in many cases badly damaged. Private sector investment had been *negative* in both 1978 and 1979.

Food, too, was a pressing problem. There was little meat, as immature cattle had been killed and whole herds smuggled across the frontier in the final weeks. There were shortages of other food —pork, chicken and eggs. Many of the urban *barrios*, where the final fighting had been fiercest, had been virtually dismembered by the Guard; and all this was merely additional to the already drastic state of material and social deprivation in which most of the people had lived under Somoza. Unemployment was around 38 per cent, illiteracy over 50 per cent; there was real hunger,[1] and housing and sanitary conditions were appalling.[2]

The immediate task was to reactivate the economy. While it was hoped to return quickly to pre-war production levels, immediate and large-scale injections of foreign aid were required to answer the urgent needs of the people. The composition of the new Government of National Reconstruction expressed the compromise on which the possibility of economic reconstruction was founded. For while it was accepted that the property of Somoza and his allies would be expropriated, it was also clear that

* Chapters 6, 7 and 8 first appeared in **International Socialism** 2:17 (autumn 1982) and were re-published in **Nicaragua: Revolution under siege** (Bookmarks 1985).

foreign aid was conditional on there being no further encroachment on the private sector. For the same reasons, economic reactivation would depend on the willingness of the bourgeoisie to participate. The price of that collaboration was 'political pluralism'.

On the other hand, the FSLN had led an armed overthrow of the state, and within a month moved to the establishment of a new army which was entirely under its control. It had the support of a population that had seized power, and identified its victory with FSLN leadership—a leadership that made it clear from the outset that pluralism would *not* mean the restoration of the private bourgeoisie to power. In fact, the FSLN employed the concept of pluralism in two different ways: on the one hand it was used to mean a sharing of power with the bourgeoisie, and a willingness to abide by the electoral rules; on the other, references were made to 'popular power' which argued that democracy was not about parliament but about grass-roots control of the political and economic process.[3] Yet the class nature of that power was left deliberately ambiguous and the issue of real control over society by the workers and peasants unresolved.

Mass involvement in the overthrow of Somoza had pointed to the *potential* for developing a mass, revolutionary organisation —but only the potential. What had unified that movement had not been any ideas concerning workers' power; nor had it been led by a revolutionary party setting out to build workers' councils or other bodies of workers' power. The only stated objective of the insurrection was the overthrow of Somoza. That much was achieved. The manner in which he was overthrown provided the opportunity for posing the issue of socialism—had the conscious leadership of the mass movement done so. Instead, the central issue posed by the Sandinistas was the problem of accumulation and national development—and the unity of the 'patriotic classes' against the traitors.

The base of the new economy was the expropriated property of Somoza. When the total was known, 20 per cent of agriculture, 25 per cent of manufacturing and 95 per cent of mining had passed into state ownership; this represented some 40 per cent of gross domestic product (GDP)—of the total goods produced in the country—and around 22 per cent of the productive capacity of the economy. Further, the nationalisation of banking and insurance, and the establishment of state control over imports and exports, gave the government the capacity to control finance and credit. That, however, was to be the limit of state ownership; in November 1979, the expropriation decree was withdrawn in order to stop further land takeovers and factory occupations.

The new economy, therefore, was a mixed economy. Its fundamental laws of motion would be those of capitalism —accumulation, the creation of surplus value, and subjection to the laws of the market. As the 1980 Plan made clear, the strategy behind the new economy was the development of the agro-export economy and the diversification of dependency. 'The Plan was designed to revitalise capitalism and to set up an important area of State ownership and State production.'[4] There is a central ambiguity in Sandinista economics—and it is one that recurs at every other level of political debate. According to Jaime Wheelock, for example, 'there is no need to control production. In reality what we are expropriating are the surpluses'.[5]

It was true that the new structures would allow the state both to appropriate a considerable part of the surplus, and to control the direction of investment through credit, subsidies and so on. Yet the bulk of production remained in the hands of the private sector, a private sector that had effectively suspended investment in the previous two years and which would continue to be unwilling to invest unless it was given guarantees that it would profit from this. The production of the surplus still depended on that sector. The withdrawal of the expropriation decree was one such guarantee, as were the extremely low interest rate credits granted by government. The new government's priority was accumulation of capital—yet much of that would be *private* accumulation in the context of a capitalist world market.

The Sandinistas argued[6] that the mixed economy had a different character in Nicaragua. Rather than control the functions of capitalism, the government controlled the surpluses produced in the economy. It was true that the old bourgeoisie no longer held state power; yet its existence as a class was guaranteed by the continuing existence of private enterprise. The immediate necessity was to generate surplus value in the economy, and social relations would have to be structured in order to realise that surplus. For the development of the productive forces still required the exploitation of labour. Although a greater proportion of profits would now pass to the state, those profits would still represent an accumulated labour power which would not be redistributed through society.

It was this task of accumulation that determined the character of the new economy. In Wheelock's view, the mixed economy guaranteed a continuing collaboration of private and state capital. Yet a condition of that relationship was the maintenance of private investment under state direction. Since the revolution, private investors (with one or two exceptions, such as the dominant sector in the sugar industry, run by the Pellas family) had been reluctant to raise the level of investment. If the private owners of capital continued to show the same reluctance, the state would almost certainly assume greater control and, eventually, direct ownership. Yet it would act under the same imperatives, and realise the same tasks of capital accumulation according to the same laws.

The latter development could take place under a banner proclaiming it to be socialism. Genuine socialism, however, lies outside the parameters of the economic alternatives for Nicaragua as they were thus put forward—for it implies the conscious direction, by a working class exercising power directly, over production. Since there was no conscious nucleus of revolutionaries arguing and organising for workers' power, however, that alternative was not even put forward within the debate, among any section of the Sandinistas.

The ambivalence was clear in the 1980 and 1981 Plans, whose basic planks were: production, austerity, national defence, self-sufficiency and a guaranteed basic living standard. Production was the first priority; the banners and posters proclaimed 'we are the citizens of struggle, in defence and in production'. The agro-export model of development recognised the historical insertion of the Nicaraguan economy into the world market. Nicaragua would continue to be an exporter of agricultural products, and would build its future industrial base on the elaboration and processing of those products. In this sense, the mixed economy simply reflected the unchanged reality of Nicaragua's existence within a world economy dominated by the laws of the market. The other part of the original programme—the diversification of dependency—set out to sever the exclusive reliance on the US[7] and to permit Nicaragua *to seek the best market conditions* for its products. Its ability to do both, however, depended on both economic and political conditions. Accumulation remained the central priority.

In essence, the Sandinista government faced the task of independent national development which the Nicaraguan bourgeoisie had been unable to carry through. Such a perspective required state intervention in the process of accumulation, and a general reduction in the costs of production—including labour —by reducing imports, the debt burden, inflation and the costs of reproduction of labour. The latter was to be achieved by lowering the general standard of living while still guaranteeing a social minimum, for example by attacking luxury or unnecessary consumption.

Central to such a strategy was raising the productivity of labour and winning acceptance for a general policy of austerity. The working class, objectively speaking, were being asked to bear the costs of accumulation. The bourgeoisie, on the other hand, while excluded from political power, were given ample encouragement to produce. In the short run, the predominant nationalism of Sandinista politics could sustain the alliance of workers and 'patriotic bourgeoisie' against imperialism—and present the need for accumulation as part of the task of national defence and the guarantee of economic development.

The FSLN gave recognition, in its internal political documents, to the class struggle, and promised a future transition to socialism. Yet the future promise was combined with a series of restraints on the development of independent class organisation, such as prohibitions on the right to strike. The postponement of class struggle to a future stage—after economic development had been achieved—posed the objective contradiction clearly. Though the state claimed to represent the working class, its strategy of collaboration with the bourgeoisie demanded the control and discipline of labour. The consolidation of the national state was clearly posed as the substitute for the construction of workers' power. State regulation of production was therefore coupled with limits on consumption.

A first priority was to provide the social services that Somoza had neglected. For the first time, a system of universal education and a national health service were established, while new housing, drainage and a water scheme laid down the infrastructure for development. Food and transport were subsidised. At the same time, this 'social wage' was put forward as an alternative to increases in money wages which, it was argued, would simply fuel inflation.

This argument met more acceptance in the countryside and among the urban poor than among the urban workers, whose organisation and traditions had brought them some material benefits even under Somoza. The policy aimed to socialise benefits, and above all to bring the most immediate advantage to the poorest sectors, who had provided Sandinismo with its social base before the revolution. Thus, an effective freeze on money wages in the urban and state sectors was coupled with an attack on differentials and a concerted attempt to raise basic living standards—as well as productivity—in the countryside.

The political dilemma was nowhere more clearly seen than in agriculture. Nicaraguan agriculture was an interlinked system of distinct forms of production: from modern, technological production to pre-capitalist subsistence farming. That system was the basis of the agro-export economy, and there was no time to reorganise it. Whatever changes took place in that system would have to guarantee the continuity of production. By the late 1970s, 40 per cent of rural workers were landless labourers, 30 per cent were smallholders, 12.7 per cent small commodity producers and 9 per cent middle and large bourgeoisie.[8] Before the revolution, 90 per cent of all credit went to large landowners, while at the other end of the scale only about 10 per cent of the rural population had permanent employment. Clearly, the landless had to be given land, yet without interrupting the process of production. New land had to be brought into production, or made more efficient, while still providing guarantees to the rural bourgeoisie.

The answer to both problems were the cooperatives. During the first two years after the revolution, land was rented out cheaply, in both state and private sector, to landless peasants organised into cooperatives. At the same time Credit and Service Cooperatives were formed to draw small and middle peasants into joint organisations through which they could gain access to both credit and state finance. The cooperatives performed both a political and an economic purpose. By June 1980, 1,327 Sandinista cooperatives had been formed and the production of basic grains rose significantly; furthermore, a step had been taken towards the elimination of seasonal unemployment. Yet a problem remained, because the incorporation of many landless peasants into production left a labour shortage in the export sector. In the short term, the gap was filled with voluntary labour; in the longer term, however, that sector would have to compete for labour—and thus create a wage incentive.

The 1981 Plan restated the priorities—but the context was different and more menacing. The redistributions of the first 18 months had been financed through foreign aid and loans. These policies now had to give way to the pursuit of accumulation. The same criteria would apply in both state and private sectors; luxury consumption was further cut and the criterion of profitability applied to state industries.[9]

In the United States, Ronald Reagan had come to power as president with a new policy towards Nicaragua: economic destabilisation. Early aid programmes had relied on the acquiescence of the Americans in the multilateral lending agencies;[10] Reagan, however, immediately cut all remaining US aid,[11] and began to impede the granting of multilateral aid.[12] The likelihood, therefore, was that all sources of external aid would be affected. The new US policy was summed up by secretary of state Haig:

> Although the Marxist government in Nicaragua might fall eventually of its own failures, the security of El Salvador requires the acceleration of the removal of the government in Managua.'[13]

Further, and despite the favourable terms originally negotiated for the repayment of the foreign debt, Nicaragua spent 65 per cent of its foreign earnings in 1980 on debt repayments and oil imports alone. Anticipated production levels in 1980 had not been reached (the shortfall in manufacturing was particularly serious) and the balance of payments was still negative.[14] At the end of 1980, the foreign debt hovered around $2 billion.

The reasons for the shortcomings in the 1980 Plan were many; in industry, disputes had cost a great deal, while imports were rising in price. Production was still far short of taking up all unused capacity, in good part because of the reluctance of the bourgeoisie to reinvest. The importance of raising production, for all these reasons, became increasingly pressing.

As the Central American revolution developed, the international context became more difficult for Nicaragua. Western Europe, with the exception of France, and Christian Democracy in Latin America were less than happy about developments in the region, and began to share the view that Nicaragua was in part responsible for the intensification of the struggle. More centrally, the US-financed growth of counter-revolutionary organisations on the Honduran and Costa Rican frontiers made national defence an urgent priority. Military spending rose significantly (figures are not declared, but 18-20 per cent of state spending would seem likely) and the burden of maintaining a standing army of 20,000 (rising to 50,000 by 1982) was added to the account. Further restrictions on imports were imposed, as well as controls on the export of capital.

On 19 July 1981, Daniel Ortega, head of the government *junta*, announced a series of new measures, principal among them an extension in the Agrarian Reform programme. The announcement had a double purpose, one economic, the other ideological. Ortega presented the decision as a response to the refusal of sectors of the bourgeoisie to participate fully in production, and as part of the programme to make Nicaragua self-sufficient in food by 1982-83—for most of the cooperatives were devoted to the production of basic grains. About 350,000 acres of land were expropriated on the grounds of neglect or inefficient use and given to workers' cooperatives, with ample credit and technical assistance provided by government. In the economic sense, therefore, the Agrarian Reform was designed to bring more land into production; that was the only criterion for determining which land would be expropriated. On an ideological level, it was part of the process of mobilising the rural population behind the government's strategy in which defence, production and austerity were intertwined in a policy for national development under hostile conditions.

The point was further emphasised in September 1981, with the Declaration of a State of National Economic and Social Emergency—which was converted into a law in March 1982. [It remained in operation throughout most of the rest of the decade, though it was suspended for the elections of 1984 and 1990.] The proportion of production still in private hands had not significantly changed in the two and a half years of revolution. According to the Report of the World Bank published in October 1981,[14] Nicaragua's economic recovery within a mixed economy depended on a significant increase in private investment. Yet the development of the counter-revolution had had the opposite effect. For the same reason, the emphasis on austerity and on sacrifice became more insistent—and was enshrined in the Emergency Laws. Relying on the mass organisations, and on its own political authority, the FSLN took further measures against non-essential consumption and against *all* threats to production, including strikes, and directed more investment into the search for alternative energy sources.

In its report, the World Bank set out the economic priorities clearly—and claimed that the Nicaraguan government agreed with its assessment. The urgent need, as they saw it, was to intensify the rate of accumulation, to limit social spending and decrease the share of the public sector in the GDP—in other words, to maintain and deepen austerity. Logically, they argued, this economic model required further incentives to private investment, both local and multi-national. Obviously the World Bank's view took for granted Nicaragua's role in the world economy, and the persistence of the mixed economy in Nicaragua itself. This view was confirmed by the Nicaraguan government—which in a document produced in March 1982 overstated the case for the mixed economy and for political pluralism to the extent of comparing the role of the FSLN to that of De Gaulle, the Mexican PRI or the Italian Christian Democrats![15]

The other side of the coin was that while the new politics of austerity could succeed only on the basis of a general consensus in sacrifice and the intensification of production, the Emergency Decrees also contained clauses limiting the right to strike and the right to public criticism, and defining a series of economic crimes and threats to state security which were open to the widest interpretation. It became counter-revolutionary to threaten the continuity of production. The immediate result was the arrest of several members of the private enterprise organisation COSEP and the minor trade union federation CAUS.

In his 1982 Economic Report,[16] *junta* member Cordoba Rivas discussed the results of the emergency. The public sector budget was nearly $100 million less than anticipated; the balance of payments was $400 million in deficit, and the social service budget had gone down from 17 per cent to 15 per cent of GDP—although the health and education services continued to develop, largely on the basis of voluntary labour.

The themes of Sandinista economics, then, were austerity, national defence and production. As international conditions worsened, and world recession was coupled with direct assaults on Nicaragua, the Sandinista government could not avoid the tasks of accumulation. The key question was what effect this combination of factors, national and international, would have on the development of the class struggle in Nicaragua. Historically, the combination of scarcity, external threat, and forced accumulation has produced regimes of a profoundly ruthless character. Yet the conditions of the Nicaraguan revolution were significant, for first of all it was a revolution made by the mass movement, secondly it was conducted within a mixed economy, in which, thirdly, the political leadership of the mass movement has assumed power directly and continued to exercise it. Yet it was doubtful that this new democracy could survive the assaults of austerity, external threat, and the implacable laws of accumulation. It could not both conduct accumulation and at the same time prepare the working classes for the class conflict that would arise from that process.

The reaction of the old bourgeoisie

When Somoza was overthrown, the bourgeoisie found itself at a significant disadvantage. It had failed to ensure an 'orderly transfer of power' within the existing social structures—and the state had been overthrown.

The new government represented the alliance of classes formed under FSLN leadership in the final weeks of the insurrection; in this sense it reflected clearly the political hegemony of the FSLN. Yet the old bourgeoisie was in no sense powerless. It did not control the state or the army, but it retained considerable economic power, as well as ideological influence through *La Prensa*, the official church and the radio stations which it still controlled. Further, it retained political influence over the middle classes, and in particular over many professionals in the state sector.

At first, the bourgeoisie judged that its economic power and influence in the international arena would allow it to resume political power. Alfonso Robelo and Violeta Chamorro remained in the government for eight months before resigning. But they underestimated the FSLN's determination to retain power in the state, just as they misjudged the extent to which mass participation in the insurrection would shape the institutions of society after the revolution. It was not, in any sense, a workers' state; nonetheless, the mass organisations provided the FSLN with instruments of mobilisation and of production. Even without workers' power, the option of the mixed economy was not the only alternative. Sandinista control of the state clearly posed another possibility: the assumption of economic as well as political control directly by the new state, which would then carry out the tasks the old bourgeoisie had proved unwilling to sustain. State capitalism was a second alternative to the mixed economy.

One of the original clauses of the FSLN's 1979 Political Programme[17] referred to the establishment of an elected Council of State in which the bourgeoisie would have a majority. By October 1979, however, the FSLN had made it clear that the composition of the Council would change, and that scheduled elections would be postponed until 1985. In the revised Council of State, announced four months later, the mass organisations, and thus the FSLN, had a permanent majority.[18]

The Sandinistas had found their first power base in the agricultural workers' union (ATC) and in the neighbourhood Defence Committees, which represented not only the sectors most directly involved in the insurrection, but also those who benefitted most directly from the redistributive measures. The other element of the worker-peasant alliance, the working class, presented more complex problems; yet the main trade union federations were all members of the bloc supporting the FSLN. The professional organisations, for their part, had not yet suffered any appreciable drop in their levels of consumption, and the new state offered expanded job opportunities to professionals and technicians. In the intense ideological struggle being waged by the state, the old bourgeoisie was not in a position to consolidate its own bloc of forces; essentially, its influence lay among the bourgeoisie itself and its strength derived from its links with imperialist interests. Yet the initially tolerant attitude of the Carter administration in the US also served to undermine any bourgeois bid for power.

This became clear in the debates around the composition of the Council of State—an argument which the bourgeoisie lost. In November 1980, COSEP members walked out of the Council of State, and in March 1981 Robelo staged a key test of bourgeois political influence. His party, the MDN, called a rally at Nandaime; as the time for the rally approached, the slogan 'Nandaime no va' (Nandaime won't happen) began to appear on every wall. Without official FSLN support, the Sandinista Youth and the local Defence Committees set up barricades and stopped the rally. The walls then announced 'Nandaime no fue' (It didn't happen).

The end of 1980 was a key moment in the course of the Nicaraguan revolution. With Reagan in the White House, the balance of class forces changed and the location of the class struggle shifted into the international arena. Reagan's policies included the active encouragement and support of counter-revolutionary groups in Honduras and Costa Rica. The new economic policies, with their emphasis on austerity, were developed in anticipation of US economic assaults; they meant a cut in luxury consumption, a more aggressive policy towards unproductive private enterprise, and a new level of popular mobilisation around the slogan of national defence. Once again, it was the mass organisations that were called into action; and it was these organisations that, as far as the old bourgeoisie was concerned, expressed most clearly the definitive shift in the base of political power in the state.

By early 1981 the old bourgeoisie no longer believed in the possibility of taking power in the state; it returned to its historical strategy of calling for direct external intervention, on the grounds that the Nicaraguan economy was in imminent danger of collapse and that the country was inexorably slipping towards communism. This was the content of a letter signed by four leading members of COSEP in September 1981,[19] and distributed among the world's press. It was a direct challenge to the government, which had just announced the State of Emergency —and it was also a response to the Anti-Interventionist Campaign within Nicaragua, organised by the FSLN as a protest against the new aggressions of the US. The COSEP members were jailed; *La Prensa* was closed for four days for contravening the censorship clauses in the Emergency Decree.

Clearly, the Emergency Decree was a response by the

Sandinista state to a new level of aggressiveness in US policy. It also provided an instrument for the further consolidation of Sandinista hegemony, and for restating the central political problem as the struggle against US imperialism. Thus the decree was directed against a bourgeoisie which, quite clearly, was acting as an agent for American policies towards Nicaragua; but it was also directed, as later events were to show, against those who raised the defence of workers' interests.

The old bourgeoisie, for its part, had developed a new international awareness. A significant section now moved behind the counter-revolution. In March, Eden Pastora, the much-lionised *'Comandante Cero'* who had led the FSLN raid on the National Palace in 1978 and commanded the all-important southern front in 1979, announced that he had 'gone over'. His argument was that the FSLN had gone Marxist and that its leaders were growing rich and excessively powerful. It was a publicity coup for the US, and a severe problem for the FSLN. Pastora was undoubtedly a popular figure, and his decision to 'follow the smell of gunpowder' and continue the revolution in Guatemala had echoes of Che Guevara's farewell to Cuba. Yet Pastora, though an important military leader, was politically naive. And no doubt part of his resentment was due to the fact that he had been given no leading military or political position in the new state.

The Pastora incident was a test of FSLN political control. His picture was removed from the museums and the galleries of heroes, and his name was no longer used—he was referred to only as 'the traitor'. People starting burning the militia cards which carried his picture, and this was then orchestrated on a national level by the FSLN. Yet the repudiation seemed widespread and genuine—and a political triumph for the FSLN.

In April 1981 Nicaragua was swept by a sense of imminent invasion; people began to build air-raid shelters and to hold their breath every time a plane flew overhead; the militias were in a state of permanent alert. In May, Robelo went to Costa Rica and announced that he had joined Pastora. His property was confiscated, and his uneasy coexistence with a state he had set out to capture came to an inevitable end. There was no doubt that the class struggle had intensified, and that the FSLN would have to respond. Its central instrument would be the mass organisations.

Chapter seven

The mass organisations and the class struggle

AFTER the revolution, the mass organisations[1] performed a double and contradictory function. On the one hand, they served as the organisers of production, the watchdogs of productivity and the ideological instruments of the state. The Defence Committees and the Sandinista Youth, for example, acted as local representatives of the FSLN, and of government. Yet they have also been described as 'instruments of socialist democracy'[2] or (by the FSLN itself) as 'organs of popular power'. If the Nicaraguan revolution was still open to further developments of the revolutionary process, if it was to become a field of *class* struggle,[3] then the key role in such a process would fall to forms of class self-organisation developed precisely to carry that struggle forward.

When the Sandinistas seized state power, they did so as the leadership of an insurrectionary movement. The composition of that movement[4] was largely the urban poor, with a predominance of the young and the very young.[5] Although the movement had thrown up a number of new forms of organisation after February 1978, they were not, by and large, the product of any long-term tradition or accumulated experience. The only sector with such a tradition—the urban working class—did not *as a class* play an active, organised part in the fighting. The most solidly based were the Civil Defence Committees, which organised distribution, medical care and self-defence in the war zones. Within the *barrios*, elementary forms of military organisation around the barricades were expressed through the Sandinista militias. In the countryside, Sandinista cooperatives emerged in the liberated zones in an effort to maintain food production.

While the FSLN, through its various tendencies, had been working in these different areas since 1975, these organisations had not existed in any real sense before 1978. The political energies of the FSLN had largely been directed, in those years, towards work within broader front organisations—the women's organisation AMPRONACS, for example, or the health workers' and teachers' unions. The FSLN's own cells, on the other hand, were extremely small and necessarily secret. They could not function as party organisations since the FSLN had no clear concept of the role or nature of the revolutionary party, and no programme for creating workers' power in a post-revolutionary society.

Historically, the FSLN had rejected the furtherance of workers' material interests as 'economism'—and for much of its existence regarded mass work solely as a form of support action for the guerrillas. Thus it had never acquired any significant influence among organised workers. While in the 1970s the FSLN had worked to organise peasants, and out of this work had built the basis of the agricultural workers' union ATC, for military reasons such work had not been sustained or consistent; in fact, in both the countryside and the urban *barrios*, the most enduring forms of grass-roots organisation were the radical Christian Base Communities, with which the FSLN worked closely, and from which it drew many of its leading members. The decision by one section of the FSLN, the Proletarian Tendency, to do systematic mass work in the urban areas had in fact led to a split—although there was agreement among all three tendencies about the importance of student work, from which many of the FSLN's experienced members also came.

Thus these pre-revolutionary forms were above all organs of struggle, which emerged and disappeared according to the largely military needs of the insurrection. They were not workers' councils on the pattern of the *soviets* of the Russian Revolution of 1917, nor new forms of workers' democracy. They expressed the generalised opposition to Somocismo, and the *potential* for self-organisation. But the political organisations which interpreted and reflected the struggle were in fact united front organisations which included sectors of the bourgeoisie.

By the final days, there were thousands of people under arms —and it was they who would form the basis of the new Sandinista

Army. Yet in July 1979, the FSLN had no more than 500 members —and a year later there were little more than 1,000. The political organisation of the working class capable of the assumption of power was still to be developed. Again, the potential for mass-based revolutionary organisation was present—but no one was arguing for it. Thus the mass organisations expressed, not the confidence and experience of a workers' movement that had tested and tasted its own power, but rather the consolidation of the relationship between that movement and the new state.

The tension was clearly expressed in the months after the insurrection. The first organisations to be formed were the Sandinista Defence Committees, modelled on the Cuban Committees for the Defence of the Revolution, but with the significant difference that they were rooted in a population with a direct and recent experience of struggle.[6] The Defence Committees were clearly designed, in the first place, to organise urban life in the immediate aftermath of Somoza's overthrow; but they were also established with the aim of cementing the relationship between the social base of insurrection and the new state.

Yet here, too, the leadership was chosen directly by the FSLN, and built from the top downwards, both nationally and locally. Further, the period immediately after the victory was one of *demobilisation*, as raising levels of production took precedence over all other activities.[7]

The Sandinista Youth had a more direct political function, organising those young people who had made up the bulk of the fighting force in the final weeks, and tying them in a more permanent way to the FSLN. For the FSLN's influence among the young was overwhelming, and it was here that the new members would come from. Equally the women's organisation AMNLAE was designed to build on the largely open work of the women's organisations before the revolution, and to reflect the leading role of women within the FSLN.

The key mass organisations, however, were those which, *after* the seizure of power, forged the political base of the Sandinista state—the worker-peasant alliance. These were the organisations of rural workers, ATC, and the Sandinista trade union federation, the CST.

The ATC was formed in April 1978, the product of work

among the landless and impoverished peasants who had gained nothing from Somoza's limited agrarian reforms and had suffered directly the weight of repression of the Somoza state. In December 1979, at its first congress, it claimed 110,000 members. The debates at the congress clearly reflected the dual priorities of the new state—the need to raise production and improve productivity, and the obligation to raise living standards in the countryside. And at the core was the question of land. The promise of land had more than anything else motivated the 40 per cent of the population that was landless. Thus, when the FSLN tried to restrain land takeovers at the end of 1979, they were met with a mass demonstration of ATC members.

Fixed low rents and the distribution of lands held by the state answered some of the immediate demands—and the Agrarian Reform Law of 1981 further extended the amount of land available for redistribution. Yet the form of organisation through which land was redistributed reflected another tension. The long-term development of export agriculture would necessarily lead to the proletarianisation of the rural labour force—as those in the state sector had already become wage labourers for whom the ATC acted as a trade union. The agrarian reform affected the production of basic grains (maize, beans, rice); but the general policy in this area was not only to render Nicaragua self-sufficient in food, but also, by 1983, to begin the export of maize to other Central American countries. Thus this sector too had to be subject to criteria of efficiency and productivity, and to an overall direction of production.

The new cooperatives acknowledged private ownership of land, but they also encouraged and asserted the collective exploitation of the land, simultaneously laying the basis for a future collectivisation of agriculture. The tension between ownership and socialisation later led to a separation of these cooperatives from other, temporary cooperatives of small and medium landowners, and the organisation of the latter into a separate organisation.

One plank of the worker-peasant alliance was therefore rapidly consolidated through the ATC. Improved general conditions of work, the right to participate in production decisions in the state sector and the cooperative structure in the private sector provided a direct link with the general economic strategy.

Yet the small and medium producers also had a crucial role to play in the production of basic grains; the guarantee of sufficient food had been a central promise in the Sandinista platform. Thus production was the key, and the private sector was given easy credit facilities and guarantees of state support in order to ensure production and encourage it to raise productivity. The irony was that this served to reinforce the rural bourgeoisie and the ATC found itself arguing for restraint and productivity, both on the question of money wages and as far as land takeovers were concerned, even though this brought direct benefit to the private sector.

The other element of the alliance presented serious problems for the Sandinistas. After the seizure of power, the FSLN faced four trade union federations, and it lacked any working-class base of its own. These federations organised only a minority of the working class—yet they had traditions and roots. Further, they had been the continuous butt of FSLN criticism over the years. While the condemnation of a repressive Somoza state had meaning for the peasantry and the urban poor, the organised working class had less experience of that direct repression. It had even won a number of concessions from Somoza, enshrined in the Labour Code and illustrated by the victory of the building workers' strike in 1973. Of the four federations, the CNT (Social-Christian) had some strength among sugar and oil refinery workers; the CUS, formed by the US union federation AFL-CIO, had a very small membership; the CGTI, linked to the Communist Party, the PSN, had a larger membership and some genuine roots in the urban working class. Yet the vast majority of workers were still unorganised.

In 1979, 343,000 people were employed in agriculture, 90,000 in industry, 228,000 in commerce and service industries, and 231,000 (28 per cent of the economically active population) were unemployed. Of these, only about 4 per cent were unionised (around 16,000 workers in all) and the bulk of these in the towns. The working class, then, was tiny and consisted overwhelmingly of workers in craft industries or small workshops. Yet politically, they were a crucial sector. The original FSLN base of support (the peasantry, student movement, and so on) did not embrace any strong organisations that might oppose the FSLN, beyond some weak bourgeois leadership. The working-class movement, however, did contain organisations with their own traditions and an organised base of their own.

Central was the PSN, whose relationship with the FSLN had always been one of open hostility. Thus, in 1977, when the failure of the opposition front organisation UDEL led the PSN to reconsider its relations with the FLSN, a small section broke away, rejecting all contact with the 'petit-bourgeois adventurists' of the FSLN. This sector formed the Stalinist PCN, and its small trade union federation, the CAUS. There was another group, a pro-Chinese split from the FSLN in 1970 called the Frente Obrero; its paper, **El Pueblo**, was directed at the working class—and it had also organised an armed group, drawing in young workers and urban youth.

The FSLN's early dealings with the working class were far from successful. The Sandinista trade union organisation, the CST, was founded soon after the victory—but it did not emerge from any existing group, as the ATC had done. It was appointed by the new state, to organise the unorganised workers and to challenge the leadership of the existing organisations. Yet the CST too displayed an ambiguous role. For it was charged with organising and supervising production, and with winning the working class to the general strategy of Sandinismo. Yet part of that strategy was a lessening of differentials between country and city, a raising of the lowest wages, and a general restraint on the wage levels of the highest paid. Further, argument over this strategy was taking place in a context in which most of industry was still in private hands.

The first actions of the CST were clumsy. The first clash came with the workers at the San Antonio Sugar Refinery, who struck for a 100 per cent wage rise—and were encouraged in their strike by the Frente Obrero. The government closed down **El Pueblo**, arrested Frente Obrero members, and attempted to dissuade the strikers. In the end they granted a 30 per cent wage rise and a number of other concessions.

In January 1980, a strike by 4,000 building workers on a new park project in Managua brought the FSLN into direct confrontation with the entrenched PSN leadershp of the building workers' union. The FSLN had already attempted to seize the leadership of the building workers' union by creating a new CST organisation and arresting the PSN leader of the union when he refused to accept the manoeuvre. In early January, building workers demonstrated against the CST operation and won the release of the union leader. The strike came in response to the government's decision to lower wages and remove the annual bonus in order to provide more jobs. Wheelock, on behalf of the government, argued that the bonus had been 'a demagogic concession' on the part of Somoza. It was pointed out to him that the bonus had been won through struggle—and that the bonus and the weekly wage were the only basis for maintaining workers' living standards. The government retracted.

January and February 1980 also brought a series of strikes over wages led by the CAUS union federation—the most bitter of them at the Fabritex factory in Managua. Here the CST acted to stop the strikes, and mounted an intense campaign against CAUS which led to the sacking of several of its offices in early March.[8]

The contradiction was illustrated when a group of workers took over the El Caracol food factory in February. The reasons for the takeover were the removal of investment by the bosses and a fall in production. This takeover won immediate government approval—and was organised by the CST. Clearly, there were two concepts of trade union organisation in conflict—as continuing clashes with CAUS and Frente Obrero throughout 1980 illustrated. The new role set out for the unions through the CST was centred on production;[9] they were to oversee the raising of production and productivity, and to win the argument for austerity and sacrifice, to translate the imperatives of national defence into the workplace. But what this meant for the working class in real terms was a reduction in their standard of living.[10]

The FSLN argued that this would be compensated in two ways: through the development of the social wage, social services, and so on; and through a far greater participation in production decisions.[11] The PCN and the Frente Obrero, on the other hand, described the regime as 'bourgeois nationalist', and maintained that the role of trade unions remained the pursuit of a higher standard of living. This argument clearly had some weight, where the bulk of production was in private or state hands, and the general politics of austerity benefitted all sectors of capital equally. While the general implication was that the working class now had a leading political role in the state, the reality did not confirm that. Industry was not central to the general plan for economic development; and the working class was not in power. Even Tomas Borge recognised this, in 1981, when he asserted that:

> The Sandinista government does not want an official governmental trade union movement. What we need is a trade union organisation responsive to the interests of the workers. The working class in Nicaragua must have the right to say 'no' where appropriate and... even... the right to confront the government when it is necessary.[12]

To an extent this reflected the failure of the FSLN's attempt, early in 1980, to create a unified trade union confederation; it was also a response to the continuing working-class discontent on which the CAUS and the Frente Obrero had capitalised. But it would be disingenuous to accept Borge's argument about trade union independence. On the one hand it has to be stressed that the working class was tiny and that the unionised section of the class was smaller still. In the absence of a living force, within the class itself, arguing for and organising along class lines, it was illusory to expect class-based organisation to develop.

Furthermore, in a situation of scarcity, wage demands cannot be met. The direct benefits would not come to the workers for some time—according to the Sandinista vision—though the general perspective was a socialisation of the economy and a gradual expropriation of the private bourgeoisie.[13] Yet the rhythm of that process would not be determined by the pace of internal class struggle within Nicaragua. On the contrary, the progressive limitations on the right to strike, to criticise, or to debate the general issues of socialism, for instance as they were being posed at the time in Poland, suggested that independent class organisation was being permanently sacrificed to the immediate task of accumulation. Yet the only way in which the FSLN could win acceptance of its general perspective of a transition to socialism was by clear progress towards democracy in the workers' movement and workers' control over the economic process as a whole. In a situation of external threat, and a growing urgency in the process of accumulation, the two were and remain contradictory.

The militias were also a significant mass organisation, the tangible representation of the marriage of production and national defence. Formed in 1980, the militias were to provide a permanent reserve of civilian defence; yet their purpose was more directly political. The military uniform became a mark of political commitment, and the weekly training sessions were above all forums for political education as well as opportunities for military preparation. The militias quickly reached a membership of 100,000—for the threat of external aggression was very real. They were based in communities and workplaces, and centred on the existing mass organisations.

For socialists, the arming of the people is a central element in the struggle for socialism. Here, apparently, the working class was being provided with the capacity to defend its conquests with arms. Yet the role of the militias was deeply ambiguous. In the emergency of April 1982, the militias were charged with guarding strategic roads, bridges and such like, releasing the army for the war on the borders. Yet the arms remained under the control of the army; the mass organisations did not control and distribute them. The guns remained weapons of national defence rather than class struggle, under the control of a highly politicised but professional army.

In general terms, the role of the mass organisations has been to cement the political hegemony of the FSLN and win mass support for the initiatives and strategies of the state. It seems clear, however, that they are not mass *democratic* organisations. While they can mobilise large numbers of people around specific initiatives such as the disaster of May 1982 or the health campaigns, they still represent only a *potential* base for direct political participation. Yet they are firmly controlled, both directly by the FSLN and indirectly by the general constraints on public debate and criticism within the National Emergency Law.

For the emergency has two faces. The external threat is real enough; but the emergency also addresses itself to the urgency of accumulation, and the sacrifices that such a process is based upon. In a country with weak political traditions, facing permanent and immediate crises and a real and enduring scarcity, the solutions to each of these problems lies outside the national frontiers. Where Nicaragua finds itself at the axis of so many other economic and political forces, which it cannot control, the development of democracy could well be seen as an open door to the multiple agencies of reaction, whose assaults have intensified in the past two years [1981-82].[14] These are the conditions under which the FSLN has set out to win political hegemony.

Sandinismo has been, above all, profoundly pragmatic. Its programme of government, for example, was the product of an alliance with other social forces. The leading members of the FSLN were trained in Marxism, yet it is not a revolutionary party. The Proletarian Tendency had argued that a revolutionary party must exist before the seizure of power was possible; the Terceristas, on the other hand, held that such an organisation could be built after, and out of, the overthrow of Somoza.[15]

In the event, Somoza was overthrown and political organisation was thereafter undertaken by the state. According to various writers the tendencies were dead;[16] the FSLN had unified around a single policy. The National Directorate of the FSLN certainly presents a unanimous appearance, and is undoubtedly united around the central tasks to be fulfilled. Yet there is a contradiction at the heart of Sandinismo, which must be reflected within the leadership. It is the contradiction between, on the one hand, the defence of the national state and accumulation, and on the other hand the fulfilment of the material interests of the working masses which itself requires workers' power, socialism.

The FSLN seized power without a revolutionary organisation rooted in the masses. This was reflected in the absence in the FSLN of middle or rank-and-file members with political experience. The administration of the post-revolutionary state, therefore, rests in the hands of middle-class professionals and technocrats whose commitment to workers' power is extremely questionable. The FSLN set out to build 'popular power' *from the state downwards,* and while maintaining a tight political control.

Power derived from the general support of the masses; but the real power of the FSLN lay in its control over the army, where the most serious and sustained political education takes place. It was the army that represented the political leadership, and in style and language the FSLN's hegemony was expressed in a permanent military metaphor. Put another way, the political model was a model of command; and the role of the mass organisations was to execute decisions and strategies evolved by the National Directorate of the FSLN without debate: 'the National Directorate will command' *(Direccion Nacional Ordene)* is one of the most frequent slogans at demonstrations and political events.

This structure of leadership is reinforced by several other factors. The urgency of production made the demobilisation of the people an urgent necessity in the aftermath of insurrection—and it remained the priority in a situation of constant scarcity. The language of political loyalty was rooted in ideas of sacrifice, austerity and discipline—the fruit of a necessity which set clear frontiers on what was politically possible. The central political symbols of the FSLN, for example, are the 'heroes and martyrs' who 'didn't say they were dying for their country, but died for it' —and Nicaragua has many murdered heroes to refer to. Struggle remains the central theme—but not class struggle. Rather it is continuously posed as national, and anti-imperialist. For the politics of the Sandinista government are determined by reasons of state—by the need to maintain, where possible, an internal political alliance with the old bourgeoisie, and an external one with that same class internationally, not in the interests of a developing class struggle within the country, but in response to the imperatives of survival that beset a tiny country in a world arena.

These imperatives combine in a model of state-led politics. As scarcity becomes more pronounced, under systematic US pressure, and as international social democracy grows cold towards Nicaragua, the exhortation becomes more and more insistent, and the space for independent organisation narrows. The dominant politics is increasingly a version of 'socialism' which identifies it with the organisation of economic growth by the state rather than with workers' power; a version that is [in 1982] reinforced by the practice of Nicaragua's Russian technical advisers. Bookshops carry almost exclusively Cuban and Eastern European volumes, all of which enthusiastically emphasise the reasons of state, accumulation and discipline.

There is, however, another current within Sandinismo which rebuts the mechanistic and nationalist emphasis of Russian politics. It is represented above all by Ernesto Cardenal and Tomas Borge. Borge refers frequently in moving speeches to the New Man of the Revolution,[17] the product of new social relations, of love and cooperation. These ideas have a strength in Nicaragua, where the theology of liberation was a powerful and popular ideology among the very sectors where the FSLN laid its roots. Among the peasantry and the urban poor, the Christian Base Communities, with their philosophy of radical social action, filled the political vacuum. Hence the presence within the government of five radical priests. These ideas are most powerful in the Ministry of Culture under Ernesto Cardenal himself, which emphasises self-expression, cooperation and creativity; and within education. Cardenal's brother, Fernando, headed the 1980 Literacy Campaign, which set out to teach basic skills to 400,000 people. It was very successful, both in mobilising urban youth behind the campaign, and in consolidating the revolution in the countryside.[18] The campaign was imbued with idealism, and with an emphasis on the capacity of workers and peasants to seize control of their own lives.

The real world bears down on Nicaragua. It is tiny and impoverished; its old bourgeoisie is vengeful and provincial and, having abandoned the hope of taking power, is progressively abandoning the economy to its fate and the future to Ronald Reagan; and it stands at the heart of an area of the world where, in the view of US imperialism, the future is at stake. Nicaragua's history hangs on it as a burden—and the idealistic language of 'social production' and 'cooperation' cannot hide the implacable necessity to develop its economy out of a 'qualitative dependency'.[19] It can attempt to juggle the forces that govern that process—but it cannot control them.

Chapter eight

1982: Contradictions of the Sandinista revolution*

JUST BEFORE the insurrection in 1979, the FSLN found itself with some unexpected allies. West Germany supported a negotiated solution that included the FSLN. The Christian Democrats of Costa Rica and Venezuela decided in February 1979 to give material aid to the Sandinistas; Mexico, too, made its rejection of Somoza clear at an early stage. The Europeans saw it as an opening in the heart of the American empire—and as a potential field of influence and investment in what had hitherto been the territory of US capital.

Mexico and Venezuela, too, saw an economic possibility. Nicaragua, as it developed, would be a new market for their oil and their capital and manufactured goods. Further, the Central American revolution was developing, and Nicaragua could provide an entry into that, an even wider field of investment.

After the overthrow of Somoza, Nicaragua turned to massive foreign aid to pay for its redistributive policies. By 1981, 50 per cent of that aid was coming from Latin America and the Third World, 32 per cent from Western Europe and just over 18 per cent from Cuba and Eastern Europe. Clearly, the West was willing to finance Sandinismo, but there were conditions—the mixed economy, and political pluralism. The United States under Carter had been benevolent at first, and most of the foreign aid during the first year came from or through the United States.[1] Most of it went to the private sector, in an attempt to maintain American influence over the Nicaraguan process.

Yet at the same time, the Central American revolution was

* This chapter was written in 1982 and first published in **International Socialism** 2:17 (autumn 1982).

advancing. The US-backed coup in El Salvador, in October 1979, was designed to head off events similar to those only months earlier in Nicaragua—but it served only to expose the contradictions in El Salvador more sharply. The Nicaraguan events had already made their impact there—not in terms of a democratic experiment, but in showing the possibility of a successful seizure of power through mass insurrection. Since Chile, the tide had run firmly against radical change; Nicaragua turned the stream again.

For the Eastern bloc, Nicaragua was a problem. The USSR waited the customary few months before declaring itself, and then began to provide limited, emergency aid. Yet its position on Central America remains deeply ambiguous. The region lies within the American sphere of influence, and although the USSR is interested in splits and divisions within the American camp, it clearly does not want another Cuba—this would be much too costly and vulnerable. Economically, Nicaragua is of little interest to Russia: Russia has never imported Nicaraguan products, and the potential for Russian investment there is very limited. The USSR has its own economic crisis to settle, and its own internal politial crisis to resolve. The major area of Russian and Cuban influence in Nicaragua is in technical assistance—where the political concepts of the USSR are translated into forms of organisation and strategies for growth. Clearly, neither Cuba nor the USSR would benefit from the defeat of the Nicaraguan revolution, for this would reinforce the monolith of US imperialism under an aggressive regime.

The Nicaraguans have attempted to take advantage of their focal position in a network of relationships—diplomatic and economic—in order to ensure support for their economic strategy. The Cubans and the Russians both advised caution in dealings with the old bourgeoisie; the originality of Nicaragua was that a political bloc had been built around it which threatened Carter's attempt to forge an organisation of political control on an international level and US expansion in Europe—which suited the Russians very well.

Sandinista flexibility was a response to this delicate balance —for their primary need was the widest range of channels of aid. The Cubans and the Russians provided the technical know-how— the Cubans particularly in the military sphere. The Western

European and Latin American social democrats provided the bulk of the finance—and Libya's $100 million aid programme opened a door to the Arab world and possible alternative sources of oil.

With Reagan's entry into the White House, however, the scenario changed. Trilateralism gave way in US foreign policy to an aggressive expansionism focussed on Central America. The conflict in El Salvador was a fundamental challenge to Reagan's strategic ambitions, and he identified it as an East-West struggle on Western soil. At the same time, Reagan named Nicaragua as the source of spreading revolution—and raised the level of economic and political pressure, not only on Central America itself, but also on Nicaragua's supporters. The well-orchestrated campaign to show that Nicaragua had abandoned pluralism was directed at these erstwhile allies.

By March 1982, the elections in El Salvador marked a difficult moment in the struggle there—and for Nicaragua. In the preceding months, thousands of highly trained Salvadorean troops had been sent back from their US camps to enter combat in El Salvador. The Reagan government was moving towards restarting arms sales to Guatemala; the Rios Montt coup there in March was supposed to facilitate that. The Honduran military were being rearmed, US bases were being built there, and the Hondurans were taking an increasingly direct role in El Salvador. Costa Rica was entering a profound economic crisis from which only US aid could save it. And the CIA was granted $19 million for covert activities against Nicaragua, to add to the military support already given to the Nicaraguan counter-revolution.

In such a context, bourgeois democracy grew cooler towards Nicaragua. The crisis in the Malvinas/Falklands, however, changed the situation. Europe gave reluctant support to Britain in this conflict, but in Latin America the reaction was almost unanimously in support of Argentina. Momentarily, a Latin American alliance confronted the US. The Nicaraguans, as usual, took skilful advantage of the crisis to cement and repair their relations with Latin America. France too provided $15 million worth of arms to Nicaragua, and received a visit from Daniel Ortega in July. Herrera Campins, president of Venezuela, made an official visit to the 19 July celebrations in Masaya in 1982.

The temporary breach in US relations with Latin America favoured Nicaragua, releasing the immediate pressure and allowing the government to pay some attention to the torrential rains that caused such enormous damage in May 1982. But the response to the disaster appeal was sluggish, and by July the pressure was on again. Counter-revolutionary armed attacks grew more intense, and Somocista groups tried to take the towns of Jalapa and Puerto Cabezas, at either extreme of the Honduran border. A battle lasting for weeks across the same frontier cost 50 Sandinista lives—and the whole military structure was mobilised in anticipation of major assaults on the 19th. On the anniversary, a small plane flown by members of a counter-revolutionary organisation led by Eden Pastora and based in Costa Rica attempted to bomb the airport and came perilously close to blowing up 800,000 gallons of oil stored at the port of Corinto.

When the Malvinas/Falklands conflict was over, the US administration could have adopted a conciliatory position and tried to repair its breach with Latin America. Instead Reagan's response was the line of force, the reimposition of US domination by weight of arms. One element of such a policy was a renewed economic, ideological and military assault on Nicaragua.

Since 1979, the Sandinistas have been careful to keep open the widest network of international relationships. The result has been a diplomatic caution based on national survival; the FSLN has repeated the Russian line on Poland, abstained in the UN vote on Afghanistan, given support to the Palestinian cause and refrained from comment on internal repression in Mexico. While supporting the guerrilla struggle in Central America, it has also vigorously supported peace proposals for the region, as in Ortega's speech to the UN in March [1982]. Each set of international relationships has required specific compromises.

Yet it has also meant that Nicaragua is not yet part of the Russian bloc. Aid from Eastern Europe is considerable, but still small by comparison with aid from all other sources.[2] Russian influence and the Cuban presence are still visible but not overwhelming. Politically, this dependence for survival on a complex of international networks has emphasised and reinforced the nationalism within Sandinismo, the politics of anti-imperialism and broad internal security.

Clearly, the maintenance of external alliances implies a corresponding internal alliance of classes. Even were that to change, this would not mean the resumption of a 'temporarily suspended' class struggle. The state has its own imperatives, which have already led it to place limits on the capacity of the working classes to defend their own interests and develop their own forms of organisation to that end. The new state has already consolidated its power over economy and society, and taken on the tasks of accumulation. The development of a conscious working-class movement organised for the assumption of state power and the construction of socialism has yet to occur.

On 1 May 1982 the CST, the FSLN's trade union federation, appeared with banners demanding 'the defence of the revolution and the transition to socialism'. In his speech that day, Tomas Borge spoke of the New Man, new social relations, of an end to exploitation—but he did not mention socialism.[3] The FSLN insisted that this was an independent CST decision and not official FSLN policy.

What did 'socialism' mean in this context? For some, it was a pointer to the radicalisation of the revolution, a move, perhaps, towards further expropriations. But there was no evidence of that in the weeks that followed. Nor did it mean any changes in the nature of the mass organisations, or in the role of workers' organisations within the state. The declaration from the CST instead made specific reference to the decision to press forward certain forms of workers' participation in production, and to consolidate other benefits such as factory shops and the collective contracts. Beyond that, the changing international situation had, if anything, reinforced the existing character of Sandinismo.

It has been a constant theme of Sandinista politics that democracy means more than voting, that it means a genuine, conscious participation in the running of society—and above all economic democracy. Yet that is a very different thing from workers' power. In state capitalism—particularly in Yugoslavia for instance—and among the European reformist left, worker participation has been a central theme. Yet that participation represents an invitation to workers' leaders to administer capitalism and apply its laws and imperatives directly. Socialism, on the other hand, involves the direct control of production by the producers themselves through the organs of revolutionary democracy—and in order to realise the needs of the producers as a class. Without the organised capacity of workers to continue to struggle for their own interests and *against* management, whether private or state, the talk of a transition to socialism is little more than abstract rhetoric at best, and at worst an attempt to incorporate the working class directly into the organisation of their own exploitation. 'Participation' is not a half-way house to workers' power; on the contrary it is a way of demobilising the very struggles that are needed as a first step towards this.

In Nicaragua, as long as scarcity characterises the economy, the best situation possible would be where the mass organisations were genuine, democratic, rank-and-file organisations, with an independent capacity for political organisation and education, and the capacity to exercise increasing control over the direction of the political process. Yet today [1982], in Nicaragua, that is not their role. Two factors have ensured that: first, the urgency of national defence, labour discipline and above all of firm state control over the institutions of society. It is not only the external threat that makes this imperative; it is also the need for continuing austerity, where scarcity cannot be equally distributed; for labour discipline and higher productivity is called for in both private and public sectors.

A new political leadership is being developed, particularly within the army and the Sandinista youth; yet to talk to leading members of either organisation is an arresting experience. A broad, if mechanistic, grasp of world politics is coupled always with an almost mystical moralism, full of terms such as discipline, heroism and sacrifice, all combined in the faintly disturbing cult of the person of Carlos Fonseca, the dead founder of the FSLN. According to Ortega, there are half a million people in the mass organisations—about 20 per cent of the population. This probably reflects the best estimate of Sandinista support.

Yet the pressing necessities of state are unlikely to permit a more democratic involvement of those half million people in response to the discontent generated by deepening scarcity—on the contrary, criticism is denounced as counter-revolutionary, and participation will more and more centre on obedience, loyalty and faith in the leadership. For in the absence of a politically experienced layer of workers, of a political tradition, and under conditions which severely test the ability of any organisation or state to maintain consensus and hegemony, democracy becomes a dangerous luxury. Participation means executing decisions taken—and the predominant militarism in Nicaragua, the widespread military presence, reinforces the Command Model of politics. Sandinista attitudes to the party reflect the same ambiguity. For the moment, the FSLN remains a politico-military organisation, whose leaders wear uniform and carry guns. The party and the problem of revolutionary democracy are not discussed.

There is no possibility [in 1982] of restoration of power to the private bourgeoisie in Nicaragua—unless at the hands of direct US military intervention; there are as yet no serious challenges to FSLN leadership either in Nicaragua or within the FSLN itself. Yet there is discontent, frustration and constant talk of shortages. In the end people judge a revolution by what is on the table. Three years is a very short time to create a level of political consciousness voluntarily disposed to accepting years of sacrifice and austerity. Yet this is a country where pre-capitalist forms of society still exist, and where national unity is pursued against a background of different cultures and languages.[5]

In economic terms, there seems little possibility of an end to scarcity. The balance of payments worsened in 1981-82, the price of Nicaraguan exports on the world market fell, and external aid is becoming increasingly difficult to get. Imports have already been reduced to a minimum, and consumer goods are growing harder to find every day. The basics are assured—but barely. And the prospect for national economic development is faced with exactly the same difficulties that ensured its frustration on two previous occasions in Nicaragua's history, in 1912 and 1933. Nicaragua has not broken with the world market, only sought to renegotiate its relationship with it.

The bourgeoisie has remained until now because its profits and its economic power have been guaranteed. As the world recession deepens, and Nicaragua is further besieged, the price may become too high—and they will leave with what they can carry to make a new life with the Cuban exiles in Miami. Yet this is not 1960, when the world economy was expanding and a gradualist alternative could be used to isolate Cuba. It is 1982, and the crisis of the world system, East and West, is profound. The events in Afghanistan, Poland, and Central America represent the need of the world's ruling classes to discipline and control the system in a period of general stagnation. Nicaragua cannot escape that crisis—though it has been able to exploit some of its contradictions to its own benefit.

The future will repeat the themes of austerity and sacrifice, and the world economy will inflict its brutal laws on Nicaragua. These conditions are inimical to democracy. It is likely that the state in Nicaragua will move further towards control of the economy, as the old bourgeoisie deserts and the maintenance of production becomes increasingly the key to physical survival.

Yet Nicaragua cannot survive alone. One direction in which it may look is the Russian bloc; yet this has its own economic and political crisis, and even Cuba is looking to the world market and to foreign capital. Economically, then, the USSR has little to gain in Nicaragua. Politically, it is very unlikely that it will be prepared to confront the United States on Nicaraguan soil.

Yet this will not mean, and cannot mean, the restoration of the old bourgeoisie to power. As a class, it has lost control of the state, though it still controls part of the framework in which that state continues to exist. The working people of Nicaragua have tasted a personal and social freedom they have never known; they have rights, their children survive and even the poorest go to school. It is not socialism, not workers' power—but it is a step, and an important one, in the direction of liberation. Further—and this is the key element—that element of liberation was *won*; and thus the talk of workers' democracy and popular power have a meaning and a reality in the context of Nicaragua's revolution, a reference point in a real experience. It is more than dry rhetoric.

The laws of the system press in on Nicaragua; but the example of its revolution also points outwards. In the rest of Central America, a struggle is developing, also with a mass base. These are not guerrilla *focos*, but mass armed movements which may also one day conquer state power. For Nicaragua, that would lessen the pressure, and widen the material base and the political foundation of its survival. None of this can solve the problems of development, or absolve Nicaragua from the obligation to develop its productive forces. But it can change the conditions under which this process takes place, relieve the immediate effects of scarcity, provide a greater space for manoeuvre and perhaps lessen the extent of Russian influence. More than that, it would change the balance of class forces on a world scale again.

If the Central American revolution suffers any major defeat, however, the prospects for Nicaragua will be bleak. It would face appalling economic problems that not even the most advanced political consciousness could overcome, problems that would be beyond the control of even a developed proletarian state if it became isolated. Thus the fate of the revolution is tied to the development of the revolutionary movement beyond its borders —and that is the central political dilemma. For here, reasons of state in Nicaragua conflict with proletarian internationalism.

There is no doubt that the direct involvement of the Nicaraguan proletariat in the Sandinista revolution has been at a qualitatively higher level than, say, the Cuban revolution. Yet despite the *potential* for socialism expressed in that involvement, the prospect of a transition to socialism in Nicaragua remains remote. The international context is one crucial reason; but more significantly, the struggle for workers' power and a workers' state demands other conditions which are absent in Nicaragua.

The first such condition is the existence of a revolutionary party, rooted in the working class and presenting a political alternative to populism and petit-bourgeois nationalism. The basis for such a party would need to have been laid prior to the revolution, so that the masses entered the revolutionary process aware of the need to create their own independent organs of class power. Yet neither within the FSLN, nor outside it, was such a Leninist strategy developed. The question was posed during the factional debates of 1975-77 within the FSLN; the pressure of events and the political imposition of the Terceristas, however, ensured that it was not developed as a strategy. Thus the political nucleus around which the argument for turning the revolution in a *socialist* direction might have crystallised was absent during and after the revolution.

The objective historical context was equally unfavourable. Revolutionary socialist ideas take root in the working class movement to the extent that there exists within this movement a certain level of organisation and activity—an existing struggle against the employers. Without it the confidence and consciousness which are the foundation of workers' councils in the factories—the basic organisational form of workers' power —are simply lacking. Yet the industrial working class formed an elite under Somoza. Only 16,000 workers even belonged to trade unions. Where such a tiny number of workers have developed *trade-union* consciousness it would require a far greater development of the struggle before the mass *revolutionary* consciousness capable of creating workers' councils was reached.

Without these objective and subjective conditions the high level of mass involvement will not lead the revolution in Nicaragua towards socialism. Who, then, will be the beneficiaries? It seems unlikely that the old bourgeoisie will reassert themselves; many have already left the country and for the rest the prospects of recovery in the midst of a world recession that has brought even wealthy Mexico to the brink of disaster seem remote. This leaves the Sandinista state. Increasingly it will be forced to take upon *itself* the task of capital accumulation; the economic crisis, the need for national defence and the desertion of the bourgeoisie will ensure that. The working-class movement itself is unlikely to accept any other form of hegemony. Tragically, what this amounts to is the further consolidation of state capitalism.

Predicting the future is a dangerous and fruitless pursuit. A whole number of factors may yet intervene in Nicaragua before the new state bureaucracy is fully consolidated within the Sandinista state. Other possibilities exist: a successful US-backed counter-revolution, on the one hand; or a destruction of the state under working-class pressure on the other. Excluding these possibilities, however, (and the latter is sadly the least likely) the consolidation of the state-capitalist alternative becomes increasingly the likely outcome of the process.

The survival of the Sandinista state will therefore impose one set of pressures; the development of the class struggle will impose another. Yet there is still room and there are structures in which working-class self-organisation can develop. For revolutionaries throughout the world, solidarity—raising the political costs to be paid by any US military intervention in Central America—is not only a moral obligation but a concrete contribution to the development of the revolutionary organisation of the world working class. Only to the extent that the tide turns in favour of the Central American revolution, as a prelude to fundamental change in the rest of Latin America, will the most positive elements of the Nicaraguan revolution—its idealism, its commitment to popular power, and its identification with socialism, in however confused a form—allow the next steps to be taken on the road to workers' power.

Chapter nine
1985: Reagan tightens the noose*

IN THE past two and a half years [since the previous chapter was written], the attitude of the US government towards Nicaragua has become increasingly warlike. Financial and military aid for the border war being waged by the counter-revolutionaries, the Contras, has been stepped up, while several times the US has appeared on the verge of a direct invasion. President Reagan's asides at press conferences in March 1985 likened the Contras to the French resistance against the Nazis in the Second World War, and amounted to a virtual invitation to sabotage and open war against Nicaragua.

For its part, the Sandinista government of Nicaragua has been openly conciliatory, sending home Cuban advisors and generally disentangling itself from support for the revolution in neighbouring El Salvador—in the process exposing as a total fiction the US claim that its only concern was for 'non-interference' of the Central American regimes in each other's internal affairs. The Nicaraguan government has also shown a willingness to recognise the validity of private profit, and has accepted the onerous conditions imposed on the repayment of its international debts. The Sandinistas have repeated assurances that their regime is not socialist but 'pluralist', and held Western-style elections to back this.

Despite this, US secretary of state George Shultz has accused the Nicaraguan government of 'authoritarianism', a lack of democracy, and of being 'a Libya in our backyard'.

The reasons for the US government's obsession with

---

* Written in 1985 and first published as the final chapter of the book **Nicaragua: Revolution under siege** (Bookmarks 1985).

Nicaragua have nothing to do with 'democracy' nor with any direct US economic interests. A recent report by the Rand Corporation provided a chilling account of US motives—for the Reagan government's foreign policy is based firmly on a new version of the 'Monroe Doctrine' whose central objective is US control of the American hemisphere *whatever the cost*.

The enormous armoury displayed by the US marines in 1983 in crushing the small revolt on the island of Grenada in the Caribbean clearly demonstrated this. The New Jewel Movement, led by Maurice Bishop, was in the course of a completely destructive internal struggle when US troops were dispatched to the island. Earlier in the year a huge military exercise directed against a fictitious island group much like Grenada and the Grenadines had clearly signalled US intentions. In fact when the troops invaded there was no one to fight. The operation was a fiasco, as US troops spent a week on the tiny island trying to find the American medical students they had supposedly come to rescue.

Clearly the intention of the invasion was to announce US readiness to move to direct military intervention—a warning directed to Nicaragua. In the event, the operation's failure led to a definite shift towards the inaptly named 'low-intensity warfare' option.

The other side of the US coin has been a willingness to tolerate regimes such as those in Guatemala and El Salvador, which US politicians choose to label 'democracies' but whose governments have an appalling record of systematic murder and torture of political opponents, and the use of terror against the population. Fifty thousand people died at the hands of the state in El Salvador in the four years following 1980.

The US sees the Sandinista government in Nicaragua as a threat to its control of the American hemisphere. One US Congressman has accused Shultz and the Pentagon of 'creeping paranoia', but it is not madness which explains the actions of the Reagan administration. Rather it is a faithful defence of the interests of a capitalist class locked in a recession and seeking to protect its profits at the expense of workers across the world. In this respect the Nicaraguan revolution, whatever its exact political colouring and likely future direction, represents a threat to capitalist interests.

There are elections... and elections

On 4 November 1984 free elections were held in Nicaragua for the first time in history. They were held under intense external pressure, but were generally acknowledged to be open and honest: 85 per cent of the Nicaraguan electorate voted. Two days later less than half that percentage of the voters in the US gave Ronald Reagan his second term as president.

The Nicaraguan elections were given little attention in the popular press. Yet the day after the US election the 'discovery' of a supposed shipment of Russian arms to the Nicaraguan port of Corinto was given banner headlines throughout the world. As a news story it proved highly suspect[1]—but it gave a clear indication of future US attitudes to Nicaragua.

In the run-up to the elections, Reagan had made great play of his commitment to 'democracy in the region'. Early in 1983, a new organisation entitled the 'Democratic Community' was set up under US auspices by the military governments of Guatemala and El Salvador, supported by the government of Honduras—again effectively controlled by the military. The Democratic Community was a short-lived and transparent device, intended to provide a democratic facade for a military operation in Central America.

The elections of 1984 in Guatemala and El Salvador served a similar function. They were intended for the eyes of voters in the US, on the one hand, and to preempt the elections that had been announced in Nicaragua on the other. In both Guatemala and El Salvador lists of opposition candidates were published alongside death threats to them and their families.

In Guatemala the election of General Mejia ensured the continuation in power of a military caste which had ruled since the mid-1950s. Report after report, by Amnesty International among others, had shown the military regime guilty of the hideous and sustained torture of its political opponents. US arms sales to Guatemala had been suspended in 1979 after a group of peasant protesters had been burned alive on military orders in the Spanish Embassy in Guatemala City. Nonetheless the Guatemalans continued to receive their arms, through Israel and South Africa.

Before the elections, Reagan had nominated a paid lobbyist for the Guatemalan military, Richard Stone, as his special envoy for Central America. Now the elections provided sufficient evidence for the renewal of US relations with Guatemala—with as its backdrop a pompous public debate in the Guatemalan Congress between the military government and its loyal opposition, an extreme right-wing coalition led by Mario Sandoval, an acknowledged racist and admirer of Adolf Hitler.

The presidential elections in El Salvador were in many ways a more important test. For four years a mass resistance movement, the FDR-FMLN, had controlled some two-fifths of the country. Despite massive US financial and material aid to the Salvadorean military, which included the training of more than 15,000 special 'counter-insurgency' troops, the resistance was still able to inflict major defeats on the Salvadorean armed forces.

One reason for this was that the Salvadorean government did not have political control over the army. This lay with the extreme right-wing Arena Party and its leader Roberto d'Abuisson—the organisation that had gunned down Archbishop Oscar Romero in 1980. Likewise members of the paramilitary Treasury police had murdered four US nuns returning to missionary work in El Salvador.

The US therefore favoured the ex-mayor of the capital and Christian Democrat, Napoleon Duarte, as presidential candidate. The reasons were many—and none involved rejection of the violence and extremism proudly and publicly sustained by d'Abuisson. Unlike other Christian Democrats elsewhere in Latin America, Duarte was prepared to denounce the Nicaraguans, claiming they were responsible for the resistance in El Salvador.

In elections which, as all observers agreed, were characterised by the terrorising of the population, open corruption and large-scale abstention in the areas controlled by the resistance, Duarte was elected president. No opposition candidates to the left of Duarte had been able to present their candidacy, for fear of its being posthumous.

Whatever his political label, however, Duarte's programme was familiar. Despite his well-publicised meetings with the leaders of the FDR-FMLN, he prosecuted the war against them with the same vigour as his predecessors. US aid to his government, raised on the grounds of Duarte's new democracy, was almost entirely military, while his minister of defence, Vides Casanova, ensured the continuity of military control over civilian government. The government's policy of limited reform directed at the small farmers, combined with vicious and sustained repression, had been and remained the hallmark of US policies in the Central American region.

This was the backcloth to the US denunciation of Nicaragua's general elections, with their scrupulous observance of the rules of balance in broadcasting and publicity, even when some of the candidates of the right identified themselves publicly with the counter-revolutionary campaign that was devastating the Nicaraguan economy.

The main alliance of right-wing parties, the CDN, had first called for variations and adjustments in the Law on Political Parties. When these were granted, they called upon the Sandinistas to concede the obviously impossible demand that they embark on negotiations with the counter-revolutionaries waging a war on the borders. The presidential candidate of the CDN, Arturo Cruz, then announced his refusal to participate in the elections at the last moment, on the spurious grounds that the electoral procedures were not democratic. Just before the vote he announced his sudden conversion to the cause of the Contras!

In calling elections, conducting them democratically, and allowing universal participation, the Sandinista government had called the US government's bluff. Despite Reagan's efforts to prove the elections illegitimate, the fact is that the results gave overwhelming victory to the FSLN,[2] both in the presidency and in the Assembly. If Reagan denounced the poll, it was because the wrong side won. Yet it was clear that US policy-makers recognised from the outset that the FSLN would win an overwhelming victory, and that there was no internal political alternative that could win mass support away from the Sandinistas.

On the other hand, it was also clear that the Contras had failed to achieve their promised short-term objective of creating a 'liberated area' in Zelaya province, in the north of Nicaragua. The Contras remained divided between the forces around Eden Pastora, based in Costa Rica, and the remnants of Somoza's National Guard, operating out of Honduras. They enjoyed massive direct US government and CIA support, as well as the protection of a Honduran army swollen by the 5,000 US soldiers involved in what has come to seem a permanent military manoeuvre called 'Big Pine'.

But the Contras had succeeded in causing havoc along the

northern border, terrorising the frontier population and forcing the Sandinistas into enormous expenditure to defend the border against their attacks. In the long term, this was their objective anyway: to use the threat of invasion, incursions into Nicaraguan territory, sabotage against crops and machinery, as the spearhead of economic attrition.

There can be no doubt that the elections were a propaganda victory for the Sandinistas. At that level, they were less a mark of progress towards socialist democracy than a plebiscite, successfully demonstrating the scale of support for the FSLN.

This was obviously important if Nicaragua was to retain the support of some of the more liberal regimes in Europe and Latin America, support which was so important to Sandinista eyes. But by late 1984 these 'progressive' regimes were already fading in their support. The realities of world economic recession and the powerful disciplines of the world market had already turned the attention of the Mitterrand government in France towards its own austerity programme, while the Spanish government of Felipe Gonzalez also began to distance itself from the Central American arena. Spain was prepared to send only a low-level diplomat to attend the inauguration of Daniel Ortega as president of Nicaragua in January 1985—despite official Nicaraguan protests. The only national leader who did attend was Fidel Castro of Cuba.

Yet for all the concessions made by the Sandinistas, the elections did nothing to redress the economic or social costs imposed by the activities of the Contras, nor to win more active economic or military aid from outside Nicaragua. Both directly and indirectly the elections and the concessions that accompanied them were an expensive gesture.

This was, then, one more drain on the Nicaraguan economy, but not by any means the greatest. The government acknowledged, for instance, that the cost of Contra activity during 1984 was well over a thousand lives, a billion dollars damage to sabotaged installations, a severe impact on all areas of production, and a probable shortfall of around 25 per cent in anticipated national production levels. More important, a growing proportion of the national budget was now devoted to defence. The government itself estimated this at 25 per cent of government spending, while other observers suggested the figure was far higher.[3]

The hidden costs

The political effects of these events are far-reaching and of crucial importance. For socialists, the test of democracy is in the direct involvement and participation of the mass of people in decision-making through their independent capacity for organisation, and thus in control of their society. Manifestly, the elections did not provide any guarantee of that, nor indeed can the assurances concerning the continuing rights of private capital have brought much comfort to those who continue to assert that Nicaragua is a society making its way to socialism.

Indeed, the Sandinistas' increasingly central theme of national defence and negotiation to protect the nation's integrity has served to emphasise the contradiction at the heart of the Nicaraguan revolution. For the socialist democracy to which the Sandinistas proclaim their allegiance cannot coexist with the conciliation between classes. There can be no workers' control of society while the major part of the economy—more than 60 per cent—remains in private hands, nor while the survival of the Sandinista state requires coexistence with the bourgeoisie, both internally and internationally. Such coexistence can be bought only at the expense of those sectors of the Central American working class who are conducting a heroic struggle against their own capitalist class in El Salvador and Guatemala.

These compromises, which were dangerous possibilities in 1982, have now [in1985] become reality. The reasons lie partly in the international context of the Nicaraguan revolution, the world recession and Nicaragua's own economic weakness. They also lie partly in the political history of Sandinismo itself. Against such a background, the revolution and its survival are a tribute to the Nicaraguan workers of town and country.

Yet the state that emerged from that revolution must survive in a hostile world—and that requires bringing to the bargaining table the interests of those who sustain it in power.

US propaganda makes great play of one possible solution to the problem for Nicaragua—an increasing closeness to Russia and/or Cuba. Yet the simple and unpalatable truth is that Cuba and the Soviet Union have both made it explicit that they are not prepared to take any risks in defence of the Nicaraguan state, that the Nicaraguans must find their own means of survival without recourse to Russian or Cuban help.

There were, by early 1985, still a number of Cuban and Russian advisers in Nicaragua, though the US allegations that there were 8,000 were pure propaganda. At the height of Cuban involvement there may have been 3,000 Cubans, plus a few hundred Russian specialists. By early 1985, several hundred Cubans had been sent home in a series of gestures to foreign pressure—and after the US invasion of Grenada the Cubans were careful to make a clear distinction between their readiness to *train* the Sandinista army and state security forces and any assumption that thereby they were participating in the direct defence of Nicaragua.

As for the Russians, apart from specialist technical advisers, they had provided no more than the minimum aid necessary to cover their flank and to enable them to sustain a propaganda position against the US. The 'vast stock of arms' to which Reagan made occasional reference was firmly a Pentagon delusion.

Even if the Sandinistas had wanted to, then, they could not have turned Nicaragua into a client state of Cuba or Russia. Cuba was too anxious to protect its own position, while the Russians, returning to the picture of a world divided into 'zones of influence', were hard pushed to control their own sector, as events in Poland and Afghanistan showed. Russia had no interest in risking the security of that arrangement for Nicaragua's sake.

Fundamentally, the Sandinistas have always seen the salvation of the Nicaraguan state, and the protection of Nicaragua against the constantly threatened invasion, in an alliance of many forces combined into a broad anti-Reagan, anti-imperialist front. But this is seen as an alliance of governments, states and sections of the bourgeoisie, not an international organisation of workers.

The central instrument of this alliance is the Contadora Plan, which was evolved at the end of 1983 through a joint agreement between Mexico, Venezuela, Panama and Colombia. Essentially, it is a mutual non-intervention agreement, and it is still the basis for negotiation according to the US State Department's most recent comments. According to the Plan, an agreement to expel all foreign forces from the region would provide a basis for negotiation, and bring an end to hostilities. (Presumably the actual figures involved would be based on fictions such as the US assertion that there are no US soldiers in El Salvador— when it is known that there were a significant number on active combat duty there!)

Nicaragua quickly announced its willingness to sign this agreement and entered secret bilateral talks with the US in the town of Manzanillo in Mexico. A number of Cuban and Russian personnel were then sent home. Crucially the Nicaraguans drew back from supporting the Salvadorean revolution and began to exercise pressure there for negotiation.

The Nicaraguan regime was suing for peace and seeking to guarantee its own survival. The many dead and injured in the struggles with the Contras, plus the high level of defence spending, are testimony to the Nicaraguan willingness to defend its independence and its territorial integrity to the death—which might explain US reluctance to embark on a direct invasion, whose costs both materially and politically might be enormous.

The Sandinistas' anxiety to end this conflict had led to a series of concessions. Inside Nicaragua the government had provided guarantees to the bourgeoisie, which still held the majority of the economy—for the proportion in state hands had changed little since the revolution of 1979. These concessions were made in the belief that the continuing support of the Nicaraguan bourgeoisie —small and powerless though it might be—was the price of international support for Nicaragua. Not only was there a general agreement to hold state intervention at the level it had reached at the end of 1979, but a series of inroads were made into the gains made by the mass of the Nicaraguan people. The bourgeoisie were given rights to 'special conditions of consumption', rights to purchase scarce goods in special dollar supermarkets, and the right to take dollars and personal wealth out of the country in order to buy consumer goods abroad.

The right to export capital is a crucial question. The Sandinistas have always insisted that the central economic guarantee was their government control over capital distribution; the bourgeoisie, it was argued, could retain its private wealth so long as it remained in Nicaragua, but would not be allowed to extract its wealth from the country. So this concession was a serious retreat.

Beyond that, by early 1985 consumer prices, even of the most basic goods, were rising consistently, and basic necessities were becoming scarce. There were severe shortages at all levels, and supermarket shelves were empty much of the time. The promise of self-sufficiency in basic foodstuffs by 1984-85 had been one more casualty of the war.

Most revealing, however, and most critical for a political analysis of the nature and direction of the Nicaraguan revolution, was the changing attitude of the Sandinista government towards that other possible alliance, the alliance of workers across national boundaries, unifying their common class struggle throughout the region and beyond. This other possible alliance would have set out to link those who had taken up arms in El Salvador and Guatemala with the working-class movements in the heartlands of the new world capitalist system—no longer Chicago or Birmingham or Hamburg, but the great industrial complexes of Mexico City, Sao Paolo or Cordoba in Argentina.

Nicaragua, however, chose to seek peace through the Contadora Plan, in a compromise solution which involved in its turn a response to the Salvadorean revolution. It was here that the contradictions expressed themselves most poignantly. The central plank of US policy was that Nicaragua was supporting, sustaining and arming the Salvadorean resistance. It is therefore particularly ironic that the Nicaraguans should publicly have distanced themselves from the armed struggle in El Salvador. That separation was a condition of the Contadora discussions.

Its effects, however, were even wider. For it implied that the extraordinary authority of the Nicaraguan revolution was now being used to support peace initiatives inside El Salvador, strengthening the social-democratic wing of the FDR-FMLN and against the revolutionaries within the FMLN. The effect was to swing the political pendulum away from class struggle and away from any extension of the revolution in Central America.

This is the paradox that socialists must confront. On the one hand, the Nicaraguan revolution offers an unparalleled example of what can be achieved by mass struggle. On the other, it is now presented as an example of a 'new realism', a willingness to negotiate within the framework of world capitalism and to accept that the limits of revolution are the frontiers of a single nation-state. The consequences of such a view are critical for every socialist whose concern is the overthrow of a capitalism whose most brutal face has been exposed in the assault on Nicaragua itself.

Nicaragua and the class struggle

Our common ground with all socialists, and indeed all democrats, is that imperialism's attempt to crush Nicaragua must be resisted at every level. The Nicaraguan revolution represented a great advance, an example of what a mass movement can achieve and how the apparently impenetrable alliance of military dictatorships serving US interests can be broken.

For Nicaraguans themselves, the revolution brought real and immediate improvements in living standards. The Literacy Campaign virtually eliminated illiteracy and continues to raise the general educational standard through voluntary labour. Health provision is vastly improved, despite the departure of 70 per cent of Nicaragua's very few doctors after 1979. The achievements of the revolution have already been documented.

Yet none of these undisputed improvements justifies the description of the Nicaraguan state as a workers' and peasants' government, pursuing the transition towards socialism. Those socialists who argue this position assert that Nicaraguan socialism is of a new and different kind, a 'new democracy' characterised by 'socialist pluralism'.

A socialist society, however, is not defined by its willingness to permit bourgeois opposition, but by answering the question: *which class holds power?* The Sandinistas, holding power in Nicaragua, certainly enjoyed the majority support from the mass of its people. But popularity is not the test of socialism. For socialism is the *self*-emancipation of the working class, as a result of which the workers assume power in society directly. And central to workers' control of society under socialism is their direct control of production and the organisation of the economy.

The idea that control over the majority of the production process in Nicaragua *by the bourgeoisie* is somehow of marginal or secondary importance in the country's progress towards socialism is to fly in the face of the very definition of socialism, and indeed of class itself. Classes are formed and forged in the process of production, not in the market place. To the extent that the bourgeoisie remains a class in power, directly in the economy, the state must administer a *class* society. The question 'Whose class interests does it serve?' must be at the centre of any discussion of the nature of the Sandinista state.

Equally, despite the extraordinary—perhaps overwhelming —optimism of many of the Sandinista leaders, particularly at the beginning, it would be absurd to suggest that a country of less than three million people could in any way manipulate or control the world capitalist system—when it has round its neck a $3 billion international debt, no natural resources which could render it self-sufficient, no industry to speak of, an annual balance-of-payments deficit of $400 million, and no capacity to fulfil even its most elementary needs without massive borrowing from international financial agencies controlled by its most bitter and implacable enemy. Yet some people have suggested this.

Others have claimed that the Sandinistas could, by clever manoeuvring, exploit the contradictions between the forces that are at work in the international system.[4] The reality however is otherwise. A state which must survive economically within the capitalist system must do so by raising its capacity to accumulate *at all costs*. This was doubly underlined in Nicaragua by war, imposed upon the Nicaraguans by external forces, which both determined the distribution of the country's resources and increased its need for a growing surplus simply in order to defend itself.

Does this mean that all that was necessary was to end the war? That this would then allow the march towards socialism to continue and the Nicaraguan state to devote its resources to accumulation? Only in part, for what the war had done was simply to exacerbate, to underline and emphasise, processes inherent in the relationship between Nicaragua and the world economy. These processes would be there even under conditions of peaceful coexistence.

The Nicaraguan state, in peace or in war, must face one overwhelming task: the need to accumulate as rapidly as possible in order to survive in a world economy whose laws of motion continue to be those of profitability and competition. This process of accumulation would require an *intensifying* of the exploitation of workers simply in order to extract from them a higher rate of surplus. In order to survive, the Nicaraguan state must confront the working class from which much of its support comes, as its adversary. In order to sustain the economy through the five years since the revolution of 1979, some confrontation had already taken place—ironically, to pay for the minimal concessions which had been given to the workers.

The state of emergency, first imposed in 1982, removed the right to strike, imposed press censorship and extended the state security laws. The imposition of the state of emergency was uneven: while the ban on strikes was rigidly enforced, the right-wing newspaper *La Prensa* was barely touched by censorship and allowed to continue to print its blatant alarmism and overt support for the counter-revolution.

The prohibitions against organisation were not lifted until several weeks before the 1984 election, when their removal was clearly a concession to international public opinion rather than to working-class organisation inside Nicaragua. Their removal was not intended to allow the working class to organise, but rather to allow a variety of largely bourgeois parties to take part in the election.

The battles to come

The future path of the Nicaraguan revolution is not, of course, written in the stars, or immutably fixed by the objective economic and political conditions of the world system. While the conscious political activity of any one class cannot overwhelm the objective conditions in which it finds itself, such action can affect and alter these conditions. The future of Nicaragua will be the result of a *dynamic* process, a dialectical interplay between the objective—the conditions imposed by the world capitalist system, and the subjective—the politically conscious activities of the Sandinistas, the mass movement, and, indeed, the Nicaraguan bourgeoisie.

The conclusions drawn in the last chapter, when it was written in 1982, suggested that developments in Nicaragua would lead towards an increasing appropriation of the economy by the state, towards an intensifying of accumulation, conducted directly by the state and leading ultimately towards a form of state capitalism—in which the state acts as a collective capitalist in the context of a wider world capitalist economy.

The worsening international economic and political climate, and the enormous cost to Nicaragua of the sustained military assault it has suffered, have combined to make such a process seem less likely.[5] Certainly the response of the world economy to the debt crisis of 1982-83 has been to establish more direct control over its various compartments, principally through the imposition of strict conditions for aid and debt rescheduling through the IMF. Political considerations seem to have taken second place, since Hungary, Poland, Mexico, Argentina and Britain have all been obliged to accept the same economic discipline in return for postponement of debt repayments. To this, Nicaragua can be no exception, given its deepening dependence on foreign aid.

So the Nicaraguan government's concessions to private capital are likely to continue. The range of options open to the Sandinistas are very limited. On the one hand, a form of state capitalism could emerge which, in the absence of an available 'Cuban option' (that is, large-scale and sustained Russian aid) would of necessity be more brutal, require greater austerity and involve a deepening scarcity as accumulation was conducted under the most hostile of international conditions. This would happen independently of the political will of the Sandinista leadership, and would involve them increasingly in confrontations with their own worker supporters. But it remains a possible model of growth.

The other possibility involves a return to some form of private capitalism, or at least an acceptance that state ownership will not pass its present limits, and that, in some cases, parts of the state sector will be returned to private hands. This assumes that decisions and distribution of resources in the economy will more and more be determined by international financial considerations and by the rules imposed by international financial agencies and banks.

Certainly there are no external saviours ready to rescue Nicaragua. The Russians would like nothing better than to be rid of this little 'local difficulty'. The world recession, hitting the Eastern bloc as well as the West, brought deep contradictions to the surface. Polish workers raised the issue of workers' control through the trade union Solidarity, which led to a confrontation with the state, threatening the Eastern bloc at its heart, while on the periphery the Russian army was forced to fight against a guerrilla war in Afghanistan. The parallels with Central America were no accident.

The US, for its part, would like to destroy the Nicaraguan state and restore what Reagan, in a moment of even greater than usual lunacy, described as 'the revolutionaries who were betrayed by the Sandinistas'—by which he was referring to the capitalist class which had hoped to replace Somoza and which was sitting in the wings, biting its nails and hoping the US would give it back its inheritance.

The war of attrition continues as these words are written, a war of attrition most dramatic in the armed clashes between the Contras and the Sandinistas, but whose most potent expression is the ability of the world system to impose its laws and its dynamic on *all* its component parts whatever their will to the contrary.

There are those who would argue that this is a denunciation and a betrayal of the Nicaraguan revolution. That view is not only short-sighted; it is also profoundly dangerous. Socialists are not cheer-leaders for the Nicaraguan state or any other state. We defend the Sandinista state to the extent that it represents a step forward in the struggle of the working class—the struggle to assume direct power and establish socialism on a world scale. Every such step forward must be defended and consolidated.

But this consolidation depends not on reaching a negotiated settlement with the bourgeoisie but on deepening and advancing workers' struggle itself, on recognising that the integration of the world economy does not allow any single component to declare its unilateral withdrawal.

The solution for Nicaragua does not lie in some future utopia where all contradictions are magically resolved, nor in some late-night visitation to the consciousness of one of the Sandinista leadership. It is not our task to choose factions within the FSLN leadership with which to identify or to oppose, as some sections of the left seem to believe. Workers' revolution—socialism—is not achieved on the coat-tails of another class or another country.

The Nicaraguan state, whatever its will, cannot ignore the objective factors which influence its behaviour. To argue otherwise is not only naive, it is to obscure the way that capitalism works, and therefore to disarm the working class whose interests and whose advance is the *sole* criterion for socialists.

Chapter ten

1988: The bitter price of peace*

IN MARCH 1988 the representatives of the Sandinista
government sat down across a table from the leaders of the
US-backed Contras, and agreed a ceasefire.[1] Whatever setbacks
and challenges may yet occur, it will almost certainly mark the
end of armed confrontation between the Contras and the
Sandinista army on Nicaragua's borders. [Contra attacks in fact
continued unabated right up to the 1990 elections.]

Despite the arrogant smiles worn by Contra leaders such as
Calero and Cruz, there is little doubt that they and their
paymasters in Washington had expected a different outcome.
When the US government began to assign resources directly to
the counter-revolutionaries towards the end of 1980 several
assumptions were made.[2] First, that the still disorganised and
badly equipped army of Nicaragua would not have the means to
resist the experienced and well-prepared Contras (a view that
overestimated the military skills of the corrupt and squabbling
Contra leaders and underestimated the strength of a newly
victorious Nicaraguan population). Second, that the Contras
would soon establish a bridgehead, a 'liberated territory' on
Nicaragua's Atlantic coast. And thirdly that the progress of the
war, in combination with an economic blockade and a political
assault against Nicaragua, would produce an internal political
reaction which could lead to the overthrow of the Sandinistas,
and their replacement by a coalition of church and conservative
business interests.[3]

None of these things happened. Although today [1988] the

* This chapter is taken from a longer article, 'Central America after the
Arias Plan', published in **International Socialism** 2:39 (summer 1988).

Nicaraguan economy is in a parlous state and the political, as well as the economic, consequences of the war have been profound, the Sandinistas remain firmly in power. In that sense, the Nicaraguan masses have successfully resisted the threat of invasion and defended their territorial integrity.

Yet the Nicaraguan government has consistently maintained that the war against the Contras was more than a matter of territorial defence—that it was the revolution that was at stake. And it is the fate of the revolution that will concern us here. For it is an inescapable fact that, though the Nicaraguan government claims that it has won the war,[4] it is nevertheless bargaining with the thugs and murderers maintained by the Oliver North Circus. [Colonel North was the US officer responsible for 'laundering' the undercover funds gained from arms sales to Iran and paid to the Contras by the Reagan administration. This became known as the Contragate affair.]

Furthermore the Sandinista government is offering the Contras food, housing, protection within Nicaragua and a series of political concessions. For years the Sandinistas have denounced the Contras as puppets and tools of imperialism, and as enemies they refused to recognise. Today [1988], they are not only negotiating with them, but offering them a series of guarantees which amount to political legitimacy. How can such a shift be claimed as a victory for the revolution?

In the course of the past eight years Nicaragua has lost 15 per cent of its productive capacity, some 18,000 of its citizens have died, its social welfare programmes have been indefinitely postponed and the living standards of the mass of its people have fallen significantly. Today, in 1988, its economy is more dependent on the export sector than it was eight years ago and there has been a significant reverse in the process of socialisation of the economy. Yet the most startling aspect of this period of austerity and war is that the burden of scarcity has not been evenly distributed. The Nicaraguan bourgeoisie has been shielded from its worst effects from the very outset, with privileged access to consumer goods, state subsidies to support its investments and a range of social and political privileges.

In the aftermath of peace, there is no doubt that the austerity will continue or grow worse; yet guarantees have already been provided to the middle class that its privileges will continue to be protected. How can this be reconciled with a revolution that claims (quoting the words of Sandino):

> We shall soon win the final triumph in Nicaragua, which will light the fuse of a proletarian explosion against all the imperialists of the world.[5]

The failure of the strategy of military destruction of the Sandinista state is a defeat for imperialism and a triumph for the Nicaraguans. But it tells only part of the story. If the period of open military hostility is ended, what is the nature and quality of the peace? Will it open new spaces for the development and deepening of the revolutionary process? Will the 'interrupted' Nicaraguan revolution now continue, taking up where it was suspended? Is the peace a political defeat for imperialism and the Central American ruling classes? When Reagan sent 3200 American troops to Honduras in March of this year [1988], it was in one sense a final act in the confrontation with Nicaragua. In another sense, it was the first act of the peace ushered in by the Arias Plan, contributing to the atmosphere in which negotiation will be conducted.

This plan, put forward by president Arias of Costa Rica, was agreed in its final version at the third meeting of Central American states at Esquipulas in Guatemala. Its main provisions were an end to hostilities, a political amnesty, democratisation, an end to aid to irregular forces, and an undertaking not to attack one state from another. In each country Commissions of Verification were to be set up. Essentially the plan was directed at Nicaragua, whose Commission of Verification included the inevitable Cardinal Obando. Democratisation meant establishing a parliamentary system and electoral opportunities. Nicaragua undertook to have local elections soon, and to take part in the elections to a Central American Parliament. The amnesty, of course, applied to Somocista and Contra prisoners; the democratisation to their political representatives.[6] For the working class of Central America the signs are not hopeful.

While the most hawkish of Reagan's people appear, in the wake of Contragate, to have lost ground, the Arias Peace Plan has found allies among the staunchest defenders of the interests of the American ruling class, such as Jim Wright, leader of the US House of Representatives, who has never questioned the right of the US to act in its own interests in Latin America. It is safe to assume, therefore, that leading sections of the American ruling class now believe that their objectives in Central America can now be won by economic and political means. Presumably the basis for such a conviction is that the prospects for revolution have now been driven back, allowing the emergence of political institutions and organisations that can introduce a measure of democracy without threatening the hemispheric security of the United States.

The Arias Plan is not a challenge to, but a product of, the phase of 'low-intensity warfare' initiated by the Kissinger Report of 1984,[7] the aim of military victory slowly giving way to a commitment to a political victory won against a weakened and isolated opponent.[8] The instrument of that political victory, in its turn, would be a reconstituted bourgeois democracy, controlling a strong state and secure in its ability to take on and defeat any revolutionary challenge.

The revolution and the Sandinista road

...it is very apparent that the Sandinistas in power allowed the pace and, to some extent, the direction of change in the early months after the overthrow of Somoza to be dictated by what was acceptable to their partners in the political alliance within Nicaragua and outside. Those partners were undoubtedly anxious for a return to democracy in the region, for a higher level of participation and social justice. But they were also the representatives of a reformism which represented the *alternative* to a revolutionary transformation of society. Its emphasis was, and has consistently remained, on manageable change within the framework of a world capitalist order. Thus national development is acceptable, but internationalism is not; parliamentary democracy essential, but rank and file democracy unacceptable.

It was very clear at the outset that the new government enjoyed overwhelming support within the country. It was on that basis that it claimed the support of other democracies, in the rather naive belief that capitalism really did play by its own rules. And for a very few weeks it seemed that such an arrangement might be possible, as the spokespeople of world social democracy, both secular and religious, added their voices to the plea that Nicaragua should be allowed to co-exist with the governing system. Certainly, it was among these sectors that the

Nicaraguans sought out their first allies, and not among the countries of the Eastern bloc or the revolutionary segments of the Latin American working-class movement. This had implications for all aspects of policy, as the withdrawal of the expropriation decree in November 1979 clearly showed.

In fact, the effort to gain acceptance in the international capitalist milieu was unlikely to succeed, despite initial, but limited, American aid—which in any case was a bargaining tool rather than anything else. The Carter administration had already thought better of its new moralism and was resuming military aid and arms sales to the military dictatorships in Guatemala and El Salvador.[9] Obviously the implications of the Nicaraguan revolution had not escaped them.

For whatever the subjective readiness of the new governors of Nicaragua to seek an accommodation with the world system, within a context of national independence, the objective implications of the Nicaraguan revolution were inescapable and far-reaching. A mass insurrection had overthrown one of the most secure links in the imperialist chain in this strategically important region. Furthermore, it had done so at a time when the workers in the weakest peripheral economies in the world system were being asked to bear a disproportionate part of the cost of the recession, where unemployment was rising to unprecedented levels and living standards, which had risen for significant numbers of workers in the early 1970s, were now falling catastrophically. The possibility of resistance, the opening of an alternative outcome to the world recession implicit in the Nicaraguan revolution, echoed beyond Nicaragua's frontiers. It was not lost on the American administration either.[10]

This implication was not directly drawn by the FSLN, whose frame of political reference was *national*. While they spoke of an 'example', they did not speak of a 'lead' or a direct interdependence of the diverse fronts in the struggle. In a sense, they argued from the outset on the basis of the *exceptionalism* of the Nicaraguan experience,[11] the absence of tradition, the unrepeatable quality of Nicaraguan history. In this sense, therefore, they were nationalists (and in that sense true to the thought of Sandino) and pragmatists, making political decisions in terms of the effect they might have on their support inside and outside the country.

The central problem, however, was that the political impact

of the Nicaraguan revolution was, as we have argued, the product of its *objective* character and circumstances. The FSLN were seen, in the euphoria of its aftermath, as the legitimate representatives of that revolution. They spoke with its enormous political authority. That contradiction is at the heart of the prevalent analysis of the Nicaraguan revolution.

The class politics of Sandinismo

...The perspective of national independence and development enjoyed a broad appeal among workers and the majority of the middle classes in Nicaragua. From the outset, the FSLN had set that combination at the heart of its strategy. As Carlos Vilas wrote:

> Class contradictions are subordinated in the current stage to the tasks of development and national defence.[12]

Its political consequence was the maintenance of a broad front of support among the middle classes. This had its direct external reflection, and perhaps explained the second reason why there was no revolutionary political challenge over the strategy of Sandinismo. As we have seen, that challenge could not have come from within Nicaragua, where the revolutionary tradition was weak and entirely subsumed within Sandinismo. But it *could* have come from the more developed and more independent forces of the revolutionary left elsewhere in the region and in particular in El Salvador. The political defeat of the revolutionary left in El Salvador removed from the political agenda any internationalist or regional perspective.

'The question of national sovereignty, rather than the task of development, has guided relations between the revolution and the bourgeoisie at least since 1983,' wrote Vilas.[13] From now on, and particularly after 1981, the perspective of the Nicaraguan revolution was the survival of the state. All other considerations were subordinated to that. It involved internal material survival and external political survival. And the strategy of Sandinismo pointed towards a successful alliance with sections of the bourgeoisie in order to ensure that survival.

Between 1981 and 1983, Sandinista policies both internally and externally were devoted first and foremost to winning the support of the bourgeoisie. But the implications were profound, though rarely discussed. For the working class of Nicaragua, for example, the material improvements that they might have anticipated were not forthcoming. The best-organised sections of the Nicaraguan working class, the urban trade unions dominated by the PSN, were subordinated in the internal reorganisation of the trade unions to newly organised sections of workers and absorbed into the CST, the Sandinista trade union federation. This was politically tied to the dominant Sandinista leadership. It was the newly formed CST that continually argued for the subordination (temporary, of course) of the interests of workers to the broader needs of the survival of the state. Where this argument was won politically, it was also increasingly reinforced by legislation—the State of Emergency laws which, after 1982, prolonged indefinitely the suspension of normal trade-union activities—the right to strike, for example. The same law accorded extraordinary liberty to overt opponents among the middle classes.[14]

As US-backed aggression escalated on the borders and Contra attacks became bolder and more sustained, the nature of the Sandinista project changed imperceptibly. Its horizons were continually adjusted to the realities of siege. The economic model was agrarian and reliant in an increasingly hostile world on primary agricultural exports. From now on the costs of defence increased and drew not only resources but also labour out of the economy. In the countryside the emphasis was increasingly on productivity.

The other face of the reform was a movement towards granting private, individual land ownership. The original prospect of state farms and cooperatives was adjusted to the urgent necessities of food production. The disaffection of the peasantry was addressed, in the long term, by land redistribution increasingly tilted in the direction of individual or family titles and away from cooperative or collective forms.[15] There has been a shift of resources to the countryside and it is the rural sector which now enjoys the leading position in the economy. This has been a response in part to a series of immediate necessities: the need to relocate the refugees from the attacks of the Contras, the need to raise food production for internal consumption, and the almost complete blockade on external economic aid.

No one denies the extraordinary pressure that the revolution is under. No socialist can hesitate in condemning the callousness of an imperialism that is prepared to foment hunger and distress to win a political battle. But that should not blind us to the effect on Nicaragua of these changes. The image of a fortress holding out against besieging forces does not correspond to the reality of an economy that is a constituency of a world system. Nicaragua has no energy sources; it has precious little engineering capacity; it is not an arms producer. For all of these it must turn to external agencies, which lay down conditions for their collaboration.

The original suppliers of funds to Nicaragua, the United States, have withdrawn. They have been replaced by funding agencies in Latin America (Mexico, for example, and Venezuela at first), by the support of social democracy, by other Third World support (Libya, for example) and increasingly by the Eastern bloc. But the Russians do not give without return. In January 1988 they cut off oil supplies because Nicaragua was unable to pay.

That is the context in which Nicaragua's economy has become a survival economy. But the costs of survival are borne by the working class. While the American military threat has been held off, the logic of war has taken absolute priority. The slogan 'Nicaragua must survive' is one we all echo. But the implications of survival for the working class of Nicaragua are a question that every socialist must address. And if the war has not been won, the costs have been huge. At the negotiating table Nicaragua knows that the hostile environment of the world economy offers no safe or secure corner where it can hide, no alliance that will offer a possibility of survival without compromise. The price of peace is a future collaboration with a world capitalism that will impose its own terms and conditions. Nicaragua has no one to turn to to mitigate the cost. The working class will have to bear it alone.

The price, and who is paying it

If Nicaragua has held off invasion, and it has, the permanent costs have been enormous, both economically and politically. The economy is devastated. The war has destroyed 15 per cent of productive capacity and channelled 50 per cent of the national budget towards military spending. Since 1983, when the US imposed a total embargo on aid through the international financial agencies, shortages have grown increasingly dire and consumer goods, even the most basic, have been absent for months at a time. Food production has been maintained, but at a cost. For the original agrarian programme of redistribution, with an emphasis on cooperatives and collective ownership, has given way almost completely to the distribution of land under individual titles.

More important, the original commitment to development, a diversification of the economy and growth have been wiped off the agenda by the sustained aggression of the United States and its surrogates. The economic policy that is possible in such circumstances, with a terrible irony, can only rest on the return to dependence upon the export of basic agricultural goods, particularly coffee, to the world market. Thus is 1988 the proportion of GDP deriving from agro-exports is *greater* than it was in 1980. Even so, the balance of external aid and the unwillingness of the bourgeoisie to invest, despite the Sandinistas' reassurances of every kind, have combined with falling world prices to produce less in export earnings than was envisaged. The shortfall must come from government subsidy and investment.

In Nicaragua what that has meant is a process of forced internal accumulation under appalling circumstances. Behind the economic terms is a brutal reality. Accumulation, since 1983, has been achieved by persuading the workers to accept greater sacrifices. Private consumption fell by over 8 per cent in 1984 alone: the real value of wages *fell* between 1981 and 1984 by some 35 per cent. The revaluation of the currency in 1987 was accompanied by a 300 per cent wage rise—but inflation was three times that figure. In such circumstances, inflation becomes a means of capital accumulation in the state, a kind of tax levied on the population.[16]

That tax, however, has not been levied equally. As the scarcity deepened, special supermarkets opened for those with dollars to spend, where consumer goods of every sort were easily available. More important, the capacity to defend living standards against the effects of austerity has not been equal either. Since 1982, a State of Emergency has existed in Nicaragua; its provisions include the right of government to suspend all civil rights, including the right to strike, and to act against subversion, internal or external.

The emergency decrees have been strictly applied to the working class; strikes have been rigorously and rapidly dealt with. The strike at the Fabritex plant in 1984 was a key, if little known, example. While working-class living standards have consistently fallen, more so since rural wages were raised after 1986 while urban wage rates were frozen, the capacity of workers to respond has been curtailed by the lack of a genuinely independent organisation defending the needs of the class.

The trade unions, dominated now by the CST, the Sandinista trade union federation, act to win the working class *to the positions of the state*. Thus, at its conference in June 1987, it was agreed that wage rises would be forgone by member unions as a contribution to the war effort. Further, a motion was put forward arguing for the suspension of a Labour Code put in place by Somoza, because it limited the length of the working day!

The bourgeoisie, on the other hand, have experienced much *less* restriction on their right to mobilise their own class interests. *La Prensa*, noised abroad as a liberal newspaper, is in fact a right-wing propaganda sheet, vigorously and vehemently opposed to the revolution and its inheritors. Yet despite its unremitting attacks on the Sandinistas, it has been closed for only a few months over the past nine years. The business organisations, chiefly COSEP, are not subject to the same restrictions as the trade unions. The spokespersons of reaction, such as Monsignor Obando y Bravo, archbishop of Managua, have operated freely and openly in their opposition to the Sandinistas.

While the government of Nicaragua has responded willingly, and often at great cost, to the external demands for greater *bourgeois* democracy, the same has not been true for the mass organisations. The 1984 presidential elections were indisputably above-board and produced a 67 per cent vote for the Sandinistas. Since then, the Sandinistas have given an undertaking to hold municipal elections within the year and elections to a Central American parliament envisaged in the Arias Peace Plan. The mass organisations, by contrast, do not enjoy leadership elections, and the leading organs of the FSLN are nominated by a national leadership that is self-appointed.

Rewriting the agenda

In a sense the Arias Plan is the culmination of a process of political containment of the Nicaraguan revolution that began after 1980. Its twin objectives were to isolate the revolution, expressed in a territorial isolation of Nicaragua, and to reimpose the political priorities of capitalism on the region.

The terms of the political process were withdrawal behind national frontiers, non-interference in the affairs of other countries, withdrawal of all foreign personnel and a commitment to the 'restoration of democracy'. The last provision must have produced hollow laughter in the secret torture chambers of Guatemala and El Salvador! But Nicaragua was the first to comply. Only Reagan's obduracy prevented the beginnings of a negotiated end to hostilities two or three years ago.

Though the war dragged on and the cost for the Nicaraguan masses rose geometrically, Nicaragua had already accepted the priorities of capitalism. Nicaragua stood for anti-imperialism, for non-interference and non-alignment, and it repeated endlessly its commitment to national independence and national unity. It espoused the value of a mixed economy. As evidence it pointed to the systematic protection of its own bourgeoisie against the effects of the war. It claimed only the right to an independent state.

The implementation of the Arias Plan will take time and no doubt face several crises. But its strengthening of the existing Central American states, their reintegration into the world economy and the removal from the political agenda of the revolutionary demands placed there by the Nicaraguan revolution of 1979, have been accepted by everyone involved, including Nicaragua. When the peace is finally signed it will mark the successful reconstruction of the political centre, and the unmistakable reimposition of its priorities.

Chapter eleven

1990: What went wrong?

THE REVOLUTION of 1979 was a beacon for the oppressed and exploited throughout the world. It showed how even the poorest among them, with the weakest of political traditions, could overthrow the most bloody of dictatorships. United and determined, the workers and peasants of Nicaragua had toppled the Somoza dynasty—and on their banner were inscribed the aspirations of oppressed and exploited people the world over: freedom from want and injustice, the right to health, adequate housing and education, the right to control over their own lives.

Once the insurrection had succeeded, the masses handed their banner to those who led their struggle, the Sandinistas—but in the eleven years that followed, the slogans on that banner changed.

It was not just poverty, hunger, austerity and war-weariness that led the people of Nicaragua to withdraw their support from the Sandinistas in the elections of 1990. They had endured all these under Somoza, and fought back. They had endured these in the years before 1984, and still voted overwhelmingly that year for the Sandinistas, and in the years that followed they had fought an increasingly brutal enemy in conditions of mounting scarcity and need. The explanation had to be looked for elsewhere; there was something more to it; another dimension.

The most obvious sign of this was visible on the streets of Managua, and increasingly so in the two years up to the elections of February 1990. The poverty, the hunger, the austerity were not equally distributed. Anyone walking around Managua would come across what were called the 'people's stores'. These were special supermarkets where the goods—basic foodstuffs and necessities—were subsidised to keep them within the range of ordinary people. Much of the time the shelves were empty: toilet paper or toothpaste would be absent for two or three months, and even the staples such as rice or coffee would become suddenly and inexplicably unavailable. But the stores were there—at least until early 1988. That's when they were closed down.

Not far from these people's stores were other shops: dollar supermarkets, full of goods—seventeen varieties of rice, eighteen varieties of coffee, nylons, audio equipment, new clothes. Jeans in the dollar supermarkets were $19 or $20 a pair; the wage of a teacher or civil servant in Managua was around $20 a month.

Around Managua, in among the wretchedness and obvious scarcity, were wealthy houses, with polished rosewood garage doors protecting big cars. Who were these privileged people who had been protected from the impact of austerity? These were the Nicaraguan middle class, the beneficiaries of the 'political pluralism' and the mixed economy so often proclaimed by the Sandinistas. There was cruel irony in Daniel Ortega's speech accepting election defeat in the early hours of Monday 27 February. For he repeated that the FSLN stood for political pluralism and the mixed economy—but made no mention of the defence of *revolutionary* gains.

The mixed economy meant that the effects of the austerity plans, scarcity and the American blockade did not fall on the private capitalist class. Their interests were protected. They continued to receive subsidy and support from the government. They were allowed bank accounts outside the country, with privileged exchange rates. The dollar supermarkets stayed open when the people's stores closed.

Not only that. In the last four or five years Sandinismo, far from being 'state socialism' of the kind denounced by Reagan and Bush, actually shifted resources back towards the private sector of the economy. Some 15 per cent of the state sector in agriculture, for instance, moved back into private hands. Of the economy as a whole, 65 per cent remained in private hands—not just those of small farmers, peasants working with their families, but large farmers, industrialists and manufacturers—and this proportion rose during 1988 and 1989. Those who remained in Nicaragua did so at the behest of and with the protection of the Sandinista government.

How was that possible? Where is the reconciliation between the interests of private capital and the mass of working people, of which the Sandinistas boasted so proudly? The answer is that there *was* no reconciliation. The interests of private capital were protected while the burden of austerity fell more and more on the working classes of Nicaragua.

The Sandinista government was, as it had itself declared a hundred times, devoted to the salvation of the national state, the protection of the national territory and the achievement of a national concensus. What did that mean in class terms? It meant that inside Nicaragua the interests of the bourgeoisie and the working class were to be reconciled, and if they were not reconcilable, then the interests of one side would have to be suppressed, in order to maintain that alliance, in the 'national interest'. Those who were called upon to pay an unequal share of the price were the workers and peasants of Nicaragua, the people who had made the revolution of 1979.

That was the inescapable consequence of the political strategy of Sandinismo. They had set their priority: the consolidation of an independent national state and a viable national economy in the context of the world system. They elected to survive within the terms of the laws that prevailed in that global order, and to accept the dynamics of accumulation, which it imposed in their most extreme form. The relationship between the state and the working class that this imposed was one of exploitation, while that between the state and the bourgeoisie, both at home and internationally, was one of compromise and negotiation. At the same time the Sandinista state had to develop the disciplines and controls that would ensure the continuing loyalty of the working classes to the state under these contradictory conditions. How could it do both?

Let's for a moment go back to 1979. Why were the Americans so agitated about the 1979 revolution? Why did Ronald Reagan, in his election broadcast in 1980, as he stood for the presidency of the United States, make *Nicaragua* a central issue in his campaign? Because it was an enormously powerful economic competitor? Hardly. It was one of the most impoverished economies in the world. Because it had a huge army threatening the United States? Only a film director with an overheated imagination could believe that.

But the 1979 revolution in Nicaragua *did* represent something dramatically important. In a period of world recession, when the solution that world capitalism offered to its economic problems meant falling living standards and structural unemployment—a deepening sacrifice to be borne by workers throughout the world—at that moment the Nicaraguan revolution took one of the most stable and secure of all military tyrannies and overthrew it.

In the aftermath of the 1990 elections commentators and analysts gleefully announced something they called 'the reverse domino theory'—the defeat of socialism on a global scale. They underlined this theory by misrepresenting the 1979 revolution as a political conspiracy of progressive states or as a military coup against the Somoza dictatorship. But it was neither of these. Somoza was overthrown by mass action and mass insurrection. That was the inspiring reality of the Nicaraguan revolution, demonstrating what we mean when we talk about the self-emancipation of workers.

In many ways the Nicaraguan revolution was the least expected. The struggle was more advanced in El Salvador; it had a longer and more bitter history in Guatemala. Nonetheless. Nicaragua had an impact on the workers of El Salvador, who launched their own insurrectionary movement a few months later in January 1980. In Guatemala the struggle already under way took encouragement and inspiration from the successful overthrow of the Somoza state.

It is more difficult to trace any direct link to the rising resistance of Mexican and Brazilian workers against the 'anti-inflation' packages and austerity programmes that threatened their living standards. But they could not fail to have been inspired by the Nicaraguan experience. In any event the actions of hundreds of thousands of Brazilian workers in occupying the huge engineering plants of Sao Paolo in 1980 were a timely reminder that the industrial heartlands of the world system were now located in Mexico and Brazil and other parts of the Third World where huge concentrations of workers mocked any assertions that the working class had ceased to exist.

These workers represented the powerful forces to which the Nicaraguan revolution could have harnessed its fate, and through which its achievement could have been deepened and extended.

That connection would not have been made automatically, however. It would have had to be consciously built by the leadership of the Nicaraguan revolution, on the basis of a politics of working-class internationalism. In the event, the politics that dominated the FSLN stood on a different foundation. It interpreted the Nicaraguan insurrection as a movement whose aspirations were expressed through nationalism—and which would be fulfilled by the successful consolidation of an independent national state. Thus, in place of something that could fuel, flame and inspire the struggle of the oppressed, they put an alliance of states. The concept of revolution was turned on its head.

In the ten years that followed, the representatives of the Nicaraguan revolution have, in a long series of negotiations, sought peace with the representatives of other states, seeking the right to exist as one state among equals in the concert of nations —not with the representatives of other workers and peasants, but with generals and dictators, bourgeois lawyers and politicians.

The logic of revolutionary nationalism led, then, to this. Internally, the interests of the working class were systematically subordinated to the national concensus. Specifically this meant that their organisations were disciplined or controlled, that the working class of country and city were vigorously encouraged to see this state as their voice and defender. Yet even its most unstinting supporters acknowledged that the role of this state was to mediate *between* the opposing interests of workers and capitalists inside Nicaragua: 'The FSLN exercises a mediating role between contending social and economic demands in the name of the state.'[1]

Those inside and outside Nicaragua who continued to insist that this state was the revolutionary representative of the workers and peasants were not only veiling the truth deliberately—they were cementing an alliance between workers and the state whose result was to disarm the workers' movement when the priorities of that state moved against the workers' interests. Thus revolutionaries found themselves having to argue that the *extension* of the private sector and the protection of bourgeois interests were somehow consistent with an extension of the revolution. The FSLN defended the existence of dollar supermarkets by suggesting that they represented 'an incentive for the best cadres'.

From the mid-1980s the slogan of the solidarity movement became 'Nicaragua must survive'. This posed a further question. At whose expense and on whose conditions would Nicaragua survive? Falling living standards and scarcity hit the workers directly; the closure of hospitals and schools and the paralysis of social programmes represented a further fall in the workers' quality of life. The 35,000 workers made redundant in the state sector were the visible face of a real unemployment rate touching 27 per cent.

The reality was that Nicaragua's survival was shaped by an international network of relationships whose condition was that the Nicaraguan capitalist class should be protected from these sacrifices, and that guarantees should be provided that the revolution would not be extended either inside or outside Nicaragua. That was the price and the nature of peace.

What was the impact on Mexican workers fighting unemployment and inflation, or Venezuelan workers protesting against the resurgence of hunger in their oil-rich country, when they saw Daniel Ortega publicly embracing members of their ruling class? It was unmistakeable: Nicaragua's survival—the survival of the Nicaraguan revolution—depended on finding a negotiated form of coexistence with their rulers. Carlos Vilas was clear on the issue: 'The question of national sovereignty... has guided relations between the revolution and the bourgeoisie at least since 1983.'[2]

The signs of that dominance have been tangible: devolution of state lands to the private sector, the cutting of working-class living standards in the pursuit of accumulation in a period of crisis, the introduction and enforcement of conscription into the armed forces. As the elections of 1990 approached, the consequences became even clearer. Daniel Ortega gave public undertakings to large-scale farmers organised in UNAG that a Sandinista government would not expropriate further land. Not only that, but the FSLN included wealthy capitalist farmers on its lists of candidates, FSLN spokespersons questioned the wisdom of state ownership, and Ortega's closest political aide, Bayardo Arce, held secret talks with UNO representatives.

In the real world this is the consequence of what the most articulate defenders of Sandinismo have called the reappropriation of nationalism: 'We need to incorporate values like liberty, equality, individual creativity, love and solidarity as well as democracy and patriotism.'[3] This is either unpardonable naivety or wilful self-delusion. When revolutionaries take up the slogans of patriotism, they automatically renounce internationalism, placing nations and not classes at the centre of history.

The pursuit of peace involved the progressive disengagement of the Nicaraguan revolution and its leadership from the struggles of workers and peasants, the exploited and the oppressed who had made that revolution and those of other countries inspired by its example. So the internal concencus between the middle class and the working class within Nicaragua, which has meant ever greater sacrifice for the workers and peasants, has reflected exactly a concensus on the international scene.

Late in 1989, at a summit meeting in San José in Costa Rica between the foreign ministers and presidents of Central American nations, the Nicaraguan government put its name to a declaration calling upon the Salvadorean revolutionaries, the FMLN, to lay down their arms in pusuit of a peace process. Their counterparts in that declaration were the representatives of the government of Alfredo Cristiani, whose ARENA party was the political expression of the death squads of the Salvadorean right—a government in receipt of US military aid far greater than its annual GDP and responsible for the deaths of more than 60,000 Salvadoreans in its war against the popular resistance.

The Nicaraguan state was prepared to denounce those who had followed its example in seeking to overthrow tyranny, adding its voice to those of their rulers 'in order that Nicaragua might survive'.

The result, by 25 February 1990, was that the mass of Nicaraguans had come to realise that this state for which they had fought, and the sacrifices that they had made and were continuing to make, would not come to their own benefit—but would benefit those who were now the leading partners in the alliance the Sandinistas had sought to build. If so many voted for UNO it was because that, at least, might bring an end to Contra aggression, when the aspirations for which they had made a revolution seemed no longer attainable.

The fact of that vote was itself a tragedy. For the Sandinistas, whatever they said on international platforms, had long since ceased to be the champions and defenders of the popular democracy that would have given the workers and peasants a real voice in the revolutionary process. Yet that too has been obscured by the confusions that surround the concept of democracy. Nuñez and Burbach, for example, suggest that Marxism has 'an ambivalent theoretical legacy on the question of democracy'.[4] Nothing could be further from the truth. Engels was unequivocal that democracy, authentic democracy, could be achieved only by the working class. Both he and Marx were equally clear that bourgeois or representative democracy, while it might be advance for workers, was not true freedom—for it left the bourgeois class firmly in power in a state forged to defend its class interests.

Implicit in the Nicaraguan revolution of 1979 was another possibility. For that revolution had enormous political authority —any revolution, no matter how limited the terrain on which it takes place, no matter how limited the objectives it can itself achieve, has this authority. Proof of the political weight of the Nicaraguan revolution is to be seen in the tremendous inspiration it was to so many in Central America and on the left in Europe and America—and in the fear it provoked among our rulers.

The workers' revolution, *any* workers' revolution, has its natural allies among the workers of other countries. The Nicaraguan revolution could have thrown its authority and its weight behind the struggles of those workers, behind the ideas of revolutionary socialism, international workers' solidarity and the growth of the international workers' movement.

What would that have meant? It would have tied the fate of the Nicaraguan revolution unequivocally to the growth, development and extension of the Salvadorean workers' movement. It would have sent an unequivocal message to the struggling workers of Mexico and Brazil. Centrally, it would have entailed a recognition that, however heroic its defence by the workers and peasants who made the revolution, this weak component of a world capitalist system could not survive *as a revolution* in isolation. It would have required an acknowledgement that that isolation could only be overcome by the proliferation of workers' struggles and by their solidarity and interdependence. Such *workers'* solidarity, of course, is founded upon conscious internationalist principles and built within the organisations of working-class struggle. These same principles will have to be called upon again in the struggles that Nicaraguan workers will now face, in the wake of UNO's victory, as they are pressed to accept new sacrifices in the name of 'national restoration'.

Did the defeat of the FSLN discredit socialist strategies, or the very name of socialism itself? Was this 'another defeat for Marxism', as the right was crowing all over the world?

The answer is no. Sandinismo was not socialism. Sandinismo was a new variety of an old set of ideas: the politics of 'socialism in one country', the politics of national development. Before Nicaragua is added to the list of those countries whose experience 'proves the futility of socialism', we should remember that the Sandinista state was not committed to a socialist strategy, but to a strategy of national survival. It is that strategy that has failed, again.

There was, and is, an alternative. It was implicit in the 1979 revolution and the inspiration it gave to other revolutionaries. The natural allies of those who fought Somoza were not the middle classes, who had only ever squabbled with the tyrant over the distribution of the spoils. They were among those who raised the level of class struggle in El Salvador under the impact of the Nicaraguan revolution. They were among the Guatemalans who took on their own brutal rulers. Crucially, they were among the vast bodies of organised workers in Mexico and Brazil whose potential power lay in their key role in a global economy.

The working class remains. It is there because it is the motor of the system. It has interests that have been made international by capitalism. Its potential was revealed but in microcosm in Nicaragua in July 1979, and that was enough to topple one dictator and provoke the American giant to ten years of aggression.

The prospect and necessity for socialist revolution remains on the historical agenda—and the example of the Nicaraguan revolution of 1979 remains there to inspire it.

Appendix
Report from Managua, August 1989
Sabby Sagall

MANAGUA is not the kind of city Europeans are used to: it is a conglomeration of distinct *barrios*, very spread out and separated by large fields. The centre remains the wasteland it became as a result of the 1972 earthquake. Somoza and his cronies pocketed the international emergency aid funds that poured into the country, his National Guardsmen even selling the blood plasma on the streets at black market prices.

Under the brutal, corrupt dynasty of the Somozas inequality was stark: in 1977, the richest 5 per cent of the population received 28 per cent of the total income whereas the poorest 50 per cent received 15 per cent. In 1975 1.5 per cent of the large landowners owned 41.5 per cent of cultivated land, while 40 per cent of the rural labour force depended on wage labour to supplement production from subsistence plots.

The agrarian population fell from 60 to 44 per cent of the total between 1960 and 1977. Overcrowded shanty *barrios* clustered on the edge of the towns. The urban working class, roughly 20 per cent of the active population in 1976, had a low level of organisation yet engaged at times in large-scale struggles.

Somoza's National Guard responded to the strikes and to the ghetto uprisings that began in 1978 with unrestrained savagery. By the time the FSLN marched into Managua on 19 July 1979, the civil war had claimed 50,000 lives.[1]

The FSLN took over a country in ruins. Three and a half million dollars remained in the bank after Somoza's depletions, foreign debt of $1600 per head was the highest in Latin America. It set itself ambitious goals, attempting to combine a far-reaching programme of social reform with economic reconstruction on the basis of a mixed economy. In 1980, a major campaign was launched to eradicate illiteracy, estimated in 1979 at 50.5 per cent of all adults. By the end of 1981, as a result of an enormously idealistic countrywide effort, penetrating even remote rural areas, illiteracy was reduced to 12 per cent. Improved health and social provision led to a decline in the infant mortality rate from 121 deaths per 1000 live births in 1979 to 65 per 1000 in 1986.[2]

The government nationalised the banks and insurance companies, the fishing industry, mines and foreign trade. It expropriated all the holdings of the Somoza family and its associates, a measure which affected 168 factories—amounting to 25 per cent of Nicaragua's industrial plant and employing 13,000 of the 65,000-strong industrial working class. Somoza's confiscated agricultural property was responsible for 20 per cent of agrarian production. Government investment averaged 20 per cent of GDP between 1980 and 1984, much higher than the average for Central America.

However, by 1982 large and medium private owners still accounted for 54 per cent of production in each of the two key areas of agriculture and manufacturing.[3] Private capital still accounted for 61 per cent of total GDP, a proportion that remained broadly the same between 1982 and 1987. The policy of the regime was to establish control over vital infrastructure, together with the financial system and foreign trade, but to leave production in the hands of private enterprise on condition production was maintained.

Since 1979, agrarian reform has been a crucial feature of the revolution, outstripping urban economic change and vital for the maintenance of support for the Sandinistas. In the first phase (1979-80), 21 per cent of all estates were expropriated. This included 42 per cent of all estates over 500 manzanas (850 acres). In the second phase (after July 1981), under pressure from the organised peasantry, land that was underused could also be confiscated.

Progress in individual land distribution was slow at the outset, contrary to the original Sandinista programme, because of the regime's wish to maintain broad national unity and to minimise the scope for conflict with the anti-Somocista bourgeoisie. Care was taken not to push the large and medium farmers into the arms of the counter-revolution. Poor peasants began to feel that their farms were threatened by the expanding state sector and that the revolution was something alien, even hostile, to the countryside. Forms of protest developed— abstention in the 1984 elections, rejection of education, production for the black market, even covert support for the Contras.[4]

From the end of 1984, the emphasis shifted towards the distribution of individual plots to landless or poor peasants or to those for whom the cooperative option was unattractive. This was the dynamic period of the reform when the largest amount of redistribution took place—according to Vilas, 78 per cent of all land distributed.[5] In 1989, therefore, individual farmers owned 66 per cent of the land, 9 per cent being owned by the large landowners, 57 per cent by the medium and small owners (120,000 families benefiting from the handing over of two million hectares or 4.9 million acres). State-owned land is down from 19 per cent in 1985 to 13 per cent in 1989, with the regime pursuing a policy of handing over state farms to cooperatives and individual peasants. In all, 45 per cent of the rural population have received land or titles to land already occupied.[6]

In 1987, 62.4 per cent of the labour force was employed outside agriculture. Historically, manufacturing accounts for about a quarter of GDP; in recent years, however, it has contracted due to acute shortages of machinery, spare parts and raw materials. The private sector has undertaken little new investment, though it still accounts for 70 per cent of industrial production, of which about 20 per cent consists of large-scale private capital while the remaining 50 per cent comprises small craft enterprises responsible for roughly 30 per cent of GDP.[7] In recent times the biggest employers—in textiles, clothing, shoes and furniture—have all cut back on employment in the face of a US trade embargo and the loss of their workforce to emigration or to the 'informal sector' of self-employed artisans and traders.[8]

The direct income (apart from the 'social wage') of the urban labour force declined sharply even before the introduction of the new economic measures in February 1988. After the revolution the unionisation of workers greatly increased, but the labour market has been badly disrupted by the war. In Managua, roughly half the workforce is now involved in the informal sector.[9] One sees men, women and children at traffic lights selling anything from cigarettes and toiletries to brake fluid and condoms. This has aggravated labour shortages in the factories and on farms at harvest time. Brigades of students, public employees and international volunteers have had to be sent out to bring in the coffee crop, often on privately owned farms.

In their first two years, the FSLN succeeded in raising GDP by 15 per cent; in subsequent years the escalating Contra war caused a severe contraction in economic activity. The trade deficit has been further exacerbated by falling world prices for some of Nicaragua's main export crops, for example cotton and sugar. By 1986 the negative trade balance had reached minus $479.3 million. The external debt reached an estimated $8.1 billion in 1988.[10] In 1988 an extremely fragile economy was further weakened by Hurricane Joan, which devastated parts of the country, ruining basic grain and export crops, and causing an estimated $840 million worth of damage.[11]

The Sandinista state grants credit and guarantees capitalist profits, not only of small but also of large and medium concerns whose owners, if they fulfil economic expectations, are described as the 'patriotic bourgeoisie'. These private owners are constantly being reassured as to their importance through regular government extolling of the twin principles of 'mixed economy and political pluralism'.

In an interview, Orlando Morales of the recently formed left-wing Movimiento de Unidad Revolucionaria (MUR) described how for years private entrepreneurs made money out of the state through subsidised credit. They would borrow from the banks at a fixed rate of interest and, with galloping inflation, would only have to repay roughly a third of the sum lent. Until the new economic policy ushered in early in 1988, the state also enabled the employers to make money at its expense through a system of differential exchange rates. The government paid a higher rate for the dollar to buy imported spare parts or raw materials and re-sold them to the bosses at a lower rate, similarly purchasing the finished product at a higher rate of exchange than that at which it re-sold it for export. 'The FSLN want to be on good terms with all classes: they give subsidies to the workers, credit to the peasants, high profits to the bosses.'

The costs of the US-inspired and funded war are harrowing. Between 1980 and 1986, Contra aggression claimed 17,500 lives.

Its total direct effect on Nicaragua's economy has been estimated at around $1000 million, the equivalent of three years' export earnings. Roughly half the state budget and 20 per cent of the economically active population have been absorbed by the defence effort. The indirect effects have probably cost the country another $3 billion. *Barricada*, the Sandinista paper, recently estimated the costs of the US trade embargo between 1983 and 1988 as $1092 million.[12]

In February 1988, the government launched a programme of economic shock treatment whose most striking feature was a devaluation of the currency, by which 1000 old cordobas were replaced by one 'new cordoba'. At the same time the state sector was rationalised and roughly 20,000 public employees were laid off.[13] Many subsidies on food and transport were abolished, together with price ceilings. Subsidies had had the effect of promoting speculation rather than production as peasants and traders bought cheap, subsidised provisions and resold them to the state at higher prices. The family of a worker who had dropped out of production because of poverty wages would buy up subsidised shoes and re-sell them on the street. The burgeoning informal sector thus gave a further twist to the inflationary spiral. One immediate effect of the abolition of subsidies and price ceilings was a 1000 per cent rise in the price of petrol. This measure, together with exploding inflation, caused wages to be reduced to 1950 levels.[14]

Domestic consumption plummeted, causing GDP to contract by 9 per cent in 1988; government income, dependent on indirect consumer taxes, dropped by 60 per cent. By 1989, Nicaragua was in the throes of a desperate economic and financial crisis. In January, the government unveiled a further package of austerity measures to fight inflation. A new devaluation of 15 per cent was accompanied by a 4.4 per cent cut in planned government spending in an attempt to bring the fiscal deficit down from 56 per cent to 13 per cent in 1989. The main savings came from further massive redundancies: 12,000 civil servants, 13,000 security police and 10,000 soldiers; in all, more than 1.5 per cent of the economically active population. Similarly, according to *Barricada*, the ministry of the interior's budget was slashed by 40 per cent, that of the defence ministry by 29 per cent. Health and education had been slashed in previous years so this year's cuts were lower.[15]

In May 1989 industry was operating at only 30 per cent of its capacity. There were additional cuts in subsidies, causing further rises in the cost of food, electricity and fuel.

However, the government seems to be winning the battle against inflation: this dropped from 125 per cent per month last December, to 20 per cent in March, rose to 62 per cent in June then fell back to 10 per cent in July. But the economy is experiencing a crash landing as soaring inflation gives way to deepening recession.[16]

How is the government's timing to be explained? It had become clear by 1986 that the Contras were not capable of winning the war. In August 1987, the Esquipulas talks were initiated by president Arias of Costa Rica and the so-called Central American peace plan launched. The Sandinistas believed the time was ripe to begin restructuring the economy. They describe the new measures as *'concertación'* (social pact) and *'compactación'* (rationalisation). The measures are ruthlessly monetarist, the bitter pill not sugared by foreign aid or loans to avoid devaluation, in contrast to other countries which have adopted similar programmes. The Sandinistas have so far refused to enter into any agreement with the IMF, although an article in **Barricada** claimed that its representatives and those of the World Bank were seen in Managua in the summer of 1988.[17]

However, according to Morales, because the FSLN is subject to the pressure of the masses it does take up an anti-imperialist stance. So however much they bend over backwards to satisfy US imperialism, Washington mistrusts them and will reject any overtures. If the US cannot overthrow the Sandinista state, it will try to transform it.

The central question is: who is being made to pay for the crisis? According to Morales, the social pact is not working. Since February 1988, the government has had to become tougher with most sections of the bourgeoisie. They no longer receive subsidised credit guaranteeing all their costs of production and covering up their inefficiency. Recently the government appropriated 40 per cent of the profits of three large coffee producers, who had bought dollars massively and then taken them out of the country instead of reinvesting. They went on production strike and the government took over their plantations. The San

Antonio sugar mill was also nationalised earlier this year. It was the country's leading company and had become a symbol for the private sector. The state takeover occurred as a result of a dramatic fall in production, from 125,000 tonnes of sugar in 1982 to only 60,000 in 1988-89. However, compensation terms were agreed.[18]

The agrarian bourgeoisie in general, however, are beneficiaries of the new programme so long as they invest. Because of the key role of foreign exchange in any economic recovery, incentives have been given to producers in vital export areas such as cotton and cattle ranching, the country's 'economic motor'. Recent concessions have been permission to receive payment in dollars for part of their export earnings and the right to take a proportion of their US currency out of Nicaragua. In addition, 50 per cent of the debt owed by smaller producers of basic crops such as rice and cereals was cancelled. They have also been granted reduced interest rates.[19]

Those who are shouldering the main burden of the crisis are the working class, especially in industry and the state sector. Unemployment threatens to exceed 30 per cent and working-class living standards are said to be dropping by 13 per cent a month, despite wage increases of 120 per cent in the state sector and 300 per cent permitted in the private sector. Some industrial workers are currently not even receiving wages but are paid in provisions. Planning minister Cuenca has urged urban workers to move to the countryside and grow food.

In an interview, Isidoro Tellez, general secretary of MAP, the left-wing Movimiento de Accion Popular (Marxista Leninista), argued that there are conflicts between the state and the private sector but that at the same time these serve to legitimise bourgeois ownership. According to Tellez, the mixed economy has meant dire poverty for the workers but privilege in the midst of crisis for the bourgeoisie and state bureaucrats. The budget cuts have visibly deepened inequality, rich elements maintaining or even improving their earnings. Clearly, in a situation of extreme scarcity, including hunger, class privileges are even less tolerable than in wealthier societies. Equal distribution of the burden of the crisis is a basic demand.

The austerity programme, however, has been accompanied by a series of strikes in defence of workers' living standards. Last

November, at the port of Corinto, dockers struck in support of a 300 per cent increase in piecework rates. A workers' commission was formed which refused to recognise the authority of the CST, the official Sandinista union federation.

Early this year [1989], there were strikes in response to the new austerity measures among textile, engineering, brewery and building workers. The demands were for wage increases and travel allowances and, in addition, a group of textile workers occupied their factory in protest against the employers' running down of capital investment . More than 56 sites were affected by the building workers' action. Moreover, the country's 35,000 teachers have recently been on strike following a 19 per cent cut in the education budget. Their demands were: salary increases, transport subsidies, health care and housing. They were persuaded to drop the salary demand but retained the others.[20]

According to Tellez, trade union freedom is restricted to the CST bureaucracy. The workers' assemblies are well controlled: 'If they elect a non-CST leadership, they must take the consequences.' Tellez also opposes the Arias Plan: 'Who is Arias? Why is Ortega kowtowing to him?'

With the Contras effectively finished as a fighting force, the US appears to be shifting its strategy from military overthrow of the regime to its continuing economic destabilisation, fanning the flames of popular discontent so as to defeat it politically. The CIA, together with large sections of the bourgeoisie, have been pumping money into the coffers of UNO, the right-wing opposition bloc (which includes the two Communist Parties), and into the right-wing media in an attempt to engineer rejection of the FSLN at the polls next February [1990]. *La Prensa*, mouthpiece of UNO, continues to spew out a daily flow of lies, distortions and false rumours. They know they are addressing a people tired of war and economic hardship, who expected Somoza's overthrow to result in economic improvement but whose living standards are in fact lower than during the dictatorship.

At the rally for the tenth anniversary of the revolution in July 1989, however, there was no doubting the enthusiasm of the 350,000-strong crowd and the popularity of the Sandinista leadership. It seems that the new economic programme was the product of weeks of consultation with both the private sector and the trade unions. Ortega, Cuenca and others claim that all sections of the people were consulted, from the highest level down. The government had listened to many complaints but people had come away from the discussions convinced that they had to continue making sacrifices.

Signs of discontent, though, are hard to ignore. **The Economist Report** quotes a poll according to which only 30.8 per cent of those questioned indicated support for the Sandinistas. Both Tellez and Morales believe the Sandinistas will win the elections, if only because of their superior propaganda machine. Perhaps it will be with a higher rate of abstention. The elections, though, will solve nothing. The long-term worry is that a continuing attempt to solve the crisis at the expense of the working class and the urban poor will alienate the masses from the revolution, resulting in, at best, electoral victory for the right and, at worst, a revival in the fortunes of the counter-revolution, despite the decision of the Central American presidents to demobilise the Contras.

The system that the US has spent several hundred million dollars trying to subvert is hardly a 'Communist dictatorship'. The state can perhaps be described as the piston in the engine of accumulation. It is controlled by the FSLN, a nationalist vanguard party that uses it to underpin and develop what is a largely private capitalist economy.

Is there an alternative? Sandinista supporters insist that the war and the US embargo have not left any room for manoeuvre outside the new economic framework. So long as the Sandinistas perceive their historical task within the narrow confines of the nation-state, alternative avenues of social reconstruction are effectively closed off. But from the wider perspective of international struggle, is there not an alternative to a policy whose logic, if not subjective intention, is getting into the IMF's good books?

Of course, the harsher the economic conditions, the narrower the range of political options. In recent years the deepening economic crisis caused by the war and the US blockade have narrowed such options for the Sandinistas. Even the Bolsheviks in Russia in the years after the 1917 revolution, under comparable conditions of civil war, industrial standstill, massive inflation, semi-starvation and payment of wages in kind, were forced to abandon their policies on workers' control and the independence of trade unions, which they had adopted before and immediately after the revolution. The decrees on workers' control, envisaged as a method by which autonomous factory committees would intervene in management decision-making, were rescinded. Factory committees were integrated into the trade union structure, which itself became part of the state.[21]

The point, however, is that the Sandinista regime itself has contributed to a narrowing of the range of options as a result of the nationalist limitations of its outlook. One hears the word 'socialism' being bandied about in official speeches, but it is hard to give this credence at other than a rhetorical level.

Of course, as fighters against the global *gendarme* of the twentieth century, the FSLN are entitled to the unqualified support of all socialists. Arguably, though, a genuinely socialist government, at the head of a newly created workers' state, would have acted differently, certainly before the Contra war began in 1982-83. An alternative to the Sandinistas' constant search for an all-class alliance would have been to attempt to widen the political horizons of the revolution beyond Nicaragua's borders, a message of solidarity to workers' movements throughout Latin America and a strengthening of organisational links with them. At the same time it would have sought to create and to strengthen democratic workers' organisations: factory committees and trade unions. Neither the CST nor the local Sandinista Defence Committees can be substitutes for elected workers' councils, accountable to the rank and file.

Against this, it is argued that had the Sandinistas carried out such revolutionary measures, the US would have gone beyond arming the Contras and actually sent in the Marines. However, it is highly unlikely that Reagan would have been able to launch such an invasion in the post-Vietnam atmosphere pervading US society in the late 1970s and early 1980s. There is no doubt that such an invading force would have faced a massive popular movement of national resistance. Clearly there would have been the danger that such a conflict might have sparked off an anti-war movement in the US itself on a scale at least equivalent to that against the Vietnam War. Secondly, in a period of deepening global recession, with its consequent growing instability, the US would have risked directly assisting the spread of revolutionary upsurges beyond Nicaragua. No doubt far-sighted members of the American ruling class, those not given so readily to Reagan's blustering rhetoric, were mindful of these twin dangers.

The fact remains, however, that for all the Sandinista attempts to appease and win over their own 'patriotic bourgeoisie', the US did arm the Contras and exhort them to subvert a popular revolution. In other words, the Sandinistas did not 'export revolution' but the US did export counter-revolution. For socialists, including Isidoro Tellez, ultimately the only way to defend the revolution is to deepen it—and only the working class and the poor peasants have an interest in doing this.

Abbreviations used in the text

(Organisations are based in Nicaragua unless otherwise stated.)

ATC: Agricultural workers' union.

CAUS: Minor trade union federation linked to Stalinist PCN.

CDN: Alliance of right-wing parties for the 1984 election.

CGTI: Trade union federation linked to Communist Party (PSN).

CIA: US Central Intelligence Agency.

CNT: Social-Christian trade union federation.

COSEP: Business and employers' organisation.

CST: Sandinista trade union federation.

CUS: Small trade union federation in Nicaragua formed by the US trade union federation AFL-CIO.

FAO: Bourgeois political coalition opposed to Somoza.

FDR-FMLN (also FMLN): Mass resistance movement, El Salvador.

FPR: Revolutionary Patriotic Front, coalition in support of Sandinista struggle against Somoza.

FSLN: Frente Sandinista, leaders of 1979 revolution, in power 1979-90.

GDP: Gross domestic product.

GPP: 1970s faction within the Sandinistas, advocating a strategy of 'people's war'.

IMF: International Monetary Fund

MAP: Movimiento de Accion Popular, revolutionary left organisation critical of Sandinistas.

MDN: National Democratic Movement, bourgeois political organisation led by Alfonso Robelo.

MUR: Movimiento de Unidad Revolucionaria, left organisation formed in late 1980s, critical of the Sandinistas.

ONU: Bourgeois political front against Somoza in the 1960s.

PCN: Breakaway Stalinist Communist Party of Nicaragua.

PLI: Independent Liberal Party.

PSN: Official, pro-Moscow Communist Party of Nicaragua.

TP: 'Proletarian Tendency' of FSLN in the 1970s, arguing for organisation within the working class.

UDEL: 1970s electoral coalition against Somoza.

UDN: National Democratic Front, coalition of former supporters of Somoza under US patronage.

UNAG: Organisation of large-scale farmers.

UNO: Coalition of right-wing political organisations headed by Violeta Chamorro, winners of the 1990 elections.

Notes

Chapter 1: THE IMPACT OF AN ELECTION

1. See W I Robinson and Kent Norsworthy, **David and Goliath: The US war against Nicaragua** (New York 1987) page 238.
2. A number of presidential candidates were presented by left-wing revolutionary organisations, including the PRT, MAP and MUR, which was a coalition of left-wing critics of the FSLN and whose candidate, the mathematics professor Moises Hassan, had been a member of the original governing *junta* after the 1979 insurrection, alongside Daniel Ortega and Violeta Chamorro.
3. On 'low-intensity operations', see Robinson and Norsworthy; on the US connection, see the carefully prepared evidence of the Christic Institute for the US Congressional Contragate hearings.
4. Robinson and Norsworthy, page 287.

Chapter 2: INSURRECTION

1. H Weber, **Nicaragua: the Sandinista revolution** (London 1981) page 49.

Chapter 3: THE RISE OF THE SOMOZA DICTATORSHIP

1. J Wheelock, *Raices indigenas de la lucha anticolonial ista en Nicaragua* (Mexico 1979).
2. J Wheelock, *Imperialismo y dictadura* (Mexico 1980). See this in general on the economic history of the country.
3. See *Apuntes para la historia de Nicaragua* (Managua 1980) volume 1, pages 57-59.
4. Compare Wheelock, *Imperialismo y dictadura*, page 68, and Selser, *El pequeno ejercito loco* (Havana 1960) chapter 1.
5. This is mentioned by Selser, whose *Sandino general de hombres libres* (Costa Rica 1979) and *El pequeno ejercito loco* are the best accounts of Sandino's life.
6. Sandino quoted in José Benito Escobar, *Ideario Sandinista* (FSLN:

Managua) page 7.

7. S Ramirez, *El pensamiento vivo de Sandino* (Havana 1980) pages 75-78. This is the best and most complete collection of Sandino's writings.
8. J Wheelock, *La mosquitia en la revolucion* (Managua 1981).
9. E Torres Rivas, 'Influencia de la crisis del 29 en Nicaragua', in Casanova (editor) *America Latina en los años 30* (Mexico 1977) pages 89-112.
10. See Selser's account of it in *Apuntes sobre Nicaragua* (Mexico 1978) pages 81-94.
11. See R Belausteguigoitia, *Con Sandino en Nicaragua* (Madrid 1934) page 181.
12. H Ortega, *50 años de lucha sandinista* (Mexico 1979) page 30.
13. See Wheelock, *Imperialismo y dictadura*.
14. Weber, **Nicaragua: the Sandinista revolution**, page 17.
15. See Alegria and Flakoll, *Nicaragua: la revolucion sandinista* (Mexico 1982) pages 128-135, and in general on Somoza, see R Millett, **Guardians of the Dynasty** (1977).
16. In fact, Vincente Lombardo Toledano, a Mexican and a key figure in the Latin American Communist movement, was *invited* by Somoza to form the PSN, the better to enable Somoza to control and contain the incipient working-class movement.
17. Selser, *Apuntes sobre Nicaragua*, page 182.
18. On this period in general see O Nuñez, *El somocismo y el modelo agroexportador somocista* (Managua 1981). There was considerable US investment in Nicaraguan cotton, as liberation movements were threatening the supply from Africa.
19. See Ramirez in *Las classes sociales en Nicaragua* (Managua 1981), pages 68-69.
20. See NACLA, **Nicaraguan report** (February 1976) pages 912.
21. See Wheelock, *Imperialismo y dictadura*, and Nuñez, *El somocismo y el modelo agroexportador somocista*.
22. Nuñez, *El somocismo y el modelo agroexportador somocista*, page 27.
23. This is described in Wheelock, *Imperialismo y dictadura*, chapters 5 and 6.
24. Nuñez, *El somocismo y el modelo agroexportador somocista*, page 89.
25. In Chile, for example, the Christian-Democrat agrarian reform had met obstacles, in the resistance of the landowning classes, which posed deeper questions of structural reform. These the Christian Democrat Party was not willing to confront—with the result that the reform was paralysed and the party began to split on the question.
26. See R Millett, **Guardians of the Dynasty**.

Chapter 4: GROWTH OF THE SANDINISTA RESUISTANCE

1. J M Blandon's *Entre Sandino y Fonseca Amador* (Managua 1980) is

the fullest general account of the attempts at armed struggle during the 1950s and early 1960s.

2. The account of his imprisonment is in P J Chamorro, *Los Somoza: estirpe sangrienta* (Mexico 1980) and *Diario de un preso* (Managua 1980).
3. See Ortega, *50 años de lucha sandinista*, pages 85-94.
4. See C Fonseca, *La Hora O* (Managua 1981) pages 20-23.
5. Fonseca, page 24.
6. Fonseca, page 26.
7. Fonseca, page 27.
8. H Ruiz, in **Sobre las crisis y las tendencias del FSLN** (1977).
9. See the account by Doris Tijerino, whose case was well-known and who endured terrible torture, in M Randall, **Daughters of the revolution** (1981). Another prisoner, Jacinto Suarez, tells his story in *Nicarauac*, number 3 (Managua, December 1980), pages 31-54.
10. On the subject of liberation theology and the role of Christians in the revolution, see *Nicarauac*, number 5 (1981).
11. J Wheelock in P Arias (editor) *Nicaragua: revolucion* (Mexico 1980) page 106.
12. See Valdivia (page 113) and Torres (page 117) in Arias, *Nicaragua: revolucion*.
13. See NACLA, **Nicaraguan Report**, pages 31-34; H Jung, 'The Fall of Somoza', in **New Left Review**, number 117 (London: September-October 1979) pages 69-89; G Garcia Marquez, *Los sandinistas* (Bogota 1980) pages 169-242 and Ruiz, *Sobre las crisis y las tendencias del FSLN*.
14. See Weber, page 60.
15. The irony is that Nicaragua had the highest *per capita* income in Central America throughout the 1960s.
16. See Selser, *Apuntes sobre Nicaragua*, pages 63-68.
17. The Editorial Nueva Nicaragua has just published [1982] two new books of testimonies on the Monimbo struggle, whose titles are not yet available.
18. See the account of the assault by G Garcia Marquez in **New Left Review** (1978).
19. See the interview with Humberto Ortega by Marta Haernecker in E Pineda, *La revolucion nicaraguense* (Madrid 1980) page 182.
20. For a general account of the rising see the books by Arias, Alegria and Flakoll, and C Nuñez, *Un pueblo en armas* (Managua 1981).
21. Ernesto Cardenal, a Trappist monk, is now [1982] minister of culture. His community on the lake of Nicaragua, Solentiname, became a centre for the theology of liberation. The 1977 San Carlos raid was launched from there, and the community was finally destroyed by Somoza's bombs in February 1978.

Chapter 5: THE U.S. DIMENSION

1. Some outrageous examples of American belief in 'manifest destiny' can be found in S Landau, **Serve the Devil** (New York 1971) volume 2.
2. See Monteforte Toledo, *Centroamérica: subdesarrollo y dependencia* (Mexico 1972) volume 1, chapter 6; see also J Dunkerley, **The long war: Dictatorship and revolution in El Salvador** (London 1982) and J Pearce, **Under the Eagle** (London 1982) chapter 2. Significantly, however, Nicaragua was at that stage the *least* tied economically to US interests.
3. This is the idea underlying Jenny Pearce's **Under the Eagle**, for example, but she does not fall into the trap that catches so many other analysts, who assume that Central America has no independent history of struggle.
4. Quoted in the CIIR pamphlet **Central America** (London 1987).
5. See M Davis' articles 'Late imperial America', in **New Left Review**, number 143 (January-February 1984) pages 6-38, and 'The left and the Democrats', in **New Left Review**, number 155 (January-February 1986) pages 5-36.
6. Carmen Diana Deere, 'A comparative analysis of agrarian reform in El Salvador and Nicaragua', in **Development and Change** (London 1982) page 28.

Chapter 6: STRATEGY FOR A NEW SOCIETY?

1. See the description by Nuñez of the people of the *barrios* of Acahulainca gathering around the waste tips from the local slaughterhouse in search of food, in Arias, *Nicaragua: revolucion*.
2. It was estimated that 75 per cent of all communicable disease in Nicaragua was the direct result of the lack of drinking water and of bad sanitation.
3. The concept of pluralism is developed in the government's **What the present US administration does not want you to know about Nicaragua** (Managua, March 1982) in the direction of bourgeois democracy; see the grass-roots' concept in C Nuñez, *Las fuerzas motrices en la revolucion* (Managua 1981).
4. R Fagen, 'Revolution and transition in Nicaragua', in **Socialist Review** (New York) number 59, volume 11, number 5 (September-October 1981) page 16.
5. J Wheelock, speech reported in **Intercontinental Press**.
6. *Sobre la problematica actual* (Managua 1982) page 14.
7. In fact Somoza had already diversified external trade relations through the 1970s, as the government acknowledges in **What the present US administration does not want you to know about Nicaragua**.
8. See Deere and Marchetti, 'The worker-peasant alliance in the first year of the Nicaraguan Revolution', in **Latin American Perspectives** 29 (Spring 1981) volume 8, number 2, page 42.
9. See **Latin American Regional Report** (London) 27 November 1981.

10. See NACLA, **Target Nicaragua** (1982).
11. See NACLA, **Target Nicaragua** (1982).
12. As advocated by the extreme right-wing Heritage Foundation in its Newsletter of 8 March 1982.
13. Quoted in Deere, in **Development and Change**.
14. See Wheelock's speech in **Intercontinental Press**.
15. **What the present US administration does not want you to know about Nicaragua**, page 84.
16. Cordoba Rivas, mimeograph (Managua, May 1982).
17. This and other documents are reproduced in Carmejo and Murphy, **The Nicaraguan Revolution** (New York 1979).
18. On the general question of Sandinismo and democracy see *Sobre la problematica actual*, pages 118-170.
19. See Report of the Centro Historic Centroamericano, *Boletin* (Managua) for October 1981.

Chapter 7: THE MASS ORGANISATIONS AND THE CLASS STRUGGLE

1. As a general introduction see *El papel de las organizacionas de masas en la revolucion* (Managua 1981), G Black, **Triumph of the people** (London 1982), chapter 12, and *Sobre la problematica actual*, pages 144-169.
2. Black, page 203.
3. The question posed by Fagen and by Kairowitz and Havens in an unpublished paper.
4. See O Nuñez, 'La ideologia como fuerza material y la juventud como fuerza ideologica', in *Estado y clases sociales* (Managua 1982).
5. Some as young as nine years old, such as the militant Luis Alfonso Velasquez, whose name was given to the first park built in Managua after the revolution.
6. See P Binns and M Gonzalez, **Cuba, Castro and socialism** (London 1983).
7. See the general discussion in Deere and Marchetti, in **Latin American Persoectives** 29, and Henry Ruiz in **Barricada**, 14 June 1982.
8. See Black, **Triumph of the people**.
9. On the general role of the trade unions, see for example, the CST's submission to the Unity Conference, '1981 debe encontrar una clase obrera unida' (Managua, December 1981), the pamphlet *Los trabajadores sandinistas y las tareas del momento* (Managua 1980) and the mimeographed education document from the CST (1981) called 'El papel de los sindicatos', among many others.
10. See the speech of C Nuñez in *Los trabajadores sandinistas*, page 10.
11. See J Wheelock, *Marco estrategico de la reforma agraria* (Managua 1981).
12. T Borge, quoted in Black, page 281.
13. See Wheelock, *Marco estratigico de la reforma agraria.*

14. That activity ranges from constant attacks across the frontier and the murder of teachers and others in isolated communities, through a huge propaganda campaign which includes numbers of newly arisen evangelical sects, all of which seem to find Reagan very close to God, to the use of the question of the indigenous peoples against the Sandinistas.
15. On the documents of the split see Garcia Marquez, *Los Sandinistas* (Bogota 1980).
16. Black, Weber and Hermione Harris in 'Two years of revolution in Nicaragua', in **Race and Class** (London, summer 1981) argue that there is constant internal debate.
17. See his speeches in *La revolucion sandinista* (Mexico 1981).
18. The education campaign is described in detail by J Bevan and G Black, **The Loss of Fear** (WUS: London 1981).
19. Wheelock in **Intercontinental Press**.

Chapter 8: CONTRADICTIONS OF THE SANDINISTA REVOLUTION

1. As J Castanada shows in his *Nicaragua: las contradicciones de la revolucion* (Mexico 1980).
2. See the Heritage Foundation's newsletter quoted above and Cordoba Rivas' 1982 Economic Report.
3. The May Day Speeches are reproduced in *Patria Libre* (Managua, June 1982).
4. Daniel Ortega in his speech at Masaya, 19 July 1982, fully reported in *Barricada*, 20 July 1982.
5. The problem of the Miskito Indians of the Atlantic Coast is a difficult one, and can be given as an example, though its history is too complex to go into here. Isolated from Managua, they grew up under the tutelage of British colonialism, an influence reinforced by the Moravian church. Their national identity, their claim to some form of autonomy, posed a serious threat to national integration—and the Sandinistas, by their own recognition, handled the problem badly at first. Unfortunately, this gave the US the opportunity to move and use the Miskitos against the Sandinistas. The claim by US secretary of state Haig that there have been massacres of Miskitos is nonsense—but they were moved from the border to settlements fifty miles into Nicaragua. The FSLN argue, with considerable reason, that it was for their own safety. A sensitive account of the issue is in **What the present US administration does not want you to know about Nicaragua**.

Chapter 9: REAGAN TIGHTENS THE NOOSE

1. Spokespersons for the Pentagon and the CIA later acknowledged that the Russian and Bulgarian ships rumoured to be carrying MiG fighters (an allegation later disproved) had been constantly monitored for three months before the sudden announcement to the press a few days after the Nicaraguan elections.

2. The election results were: FSLN 66.9 per cent of the vote; Democratic Conservatives (PCD) 13.9 per cent; Independent Liberals (PLI) 9.7 per cent; Social Christians (PPSC) 5.7 per cent; Nicaraguan Communist Party (PCN) 1.5 per cent; Pro-Moscow Communist Party (PSN) 1.3 per cent; revolutionary left (MAP) 1.0 per cent. Assembly seats: FSLN 61; PCD 14; PLI 9; PPSC 2; PSN 2; MAP 2. Of the 1.5 million registered voters, 1.2 million cast their votes.

3. See for example Peter Pringle writing in **The Observer** (London, 3 March 1985) page 13.

4. As a sophisticated statement of recent thinking in the Sandinista leadership, see the series of interviews with Jaime Wheelock republished in **Nicaragua: The great challenge** (Managua 1984).

5. This case is argued in Peter Binns' article, 'Revolution and state capitalism in the Third World', in **International Socialism** 2:25 (autumn 1984) pages 37-68. However the strengthened position of private industry in the years 1982-85 may yet prove short-lived. If aid, trade, finance, and spare parts become embargoed on a major scale by the United States and the other Western powers, then no amount of concessions by the Sandinistas are likely to keep the bulk of firms in business. The situation is already serious at the time of writing [1985]. The strangulation of the economy—partly due to the blocking of international aid, loans and trade with the United States—has produced a chronic $400 million per year shortfall on the balance of trade. Beyond a certain point the economic pressure that has led to the need to make concessions to private industry will produce a need to do the opposite—to give up on it partially or totally. A more centrally-directed war economy would then result, which would inevitably imply a state structure more akin to Cuban-style state capitalism.

Chapter 10: THE BITTER PRICE OF PEACE

1. The ceasefire agreement will provide a safe territory for the Contras within Nicaragua before final negotiations begin. Though there is some dispute about it, the Sandinista government guarantees food and provisions. The US government will continue to provide non-military aid, sent through a neutral agency. A further condition concerns the release of Contra prisoners, though details remain unclear.

2. See Robinson and Norsworthy, pages 39-79. This is probably the best account of the stategic thinking behind American government responses to Nicaragua.

3. These interests were represented by the business organisation COSEP and the ubiquitous Archbishop (now Cardinal) Obando y Bravo. Obando was a late convert to the battle to overthrow Somoza, and has since become the central figure in the coalitions of the right. When he was appointed cardinal his first mass was celebrated among the Nicaraguans—of Miama! His allegiances, therefore, are very clear. Today [1988] he is the chair of

the Conciliation Commission appointed under the Arias Plan to bring about the return to normal political life!

4. The minister of defence, Humberto Ortega, was explicit in his claim in the week of 24 April 1988 (see **The Guardian** (London)).

5. Bayardo Arce, in Invernizzi, Pisani and Ceberio, *Los Sandinistas* (Editorale Vanguardia: Managua 1986) page 14.

6. See *Envio* (published in English by the Instituto Historico Centro-américano, Apdo A-194, Managua) volume 7, number 80 (February-March 1988) pages 39-45.

7. See for example **The Economist** (London) 29 October 1983, special report on Central America titled 'The Second Spanish Civil War', pages 49-56; also Borosage, 'No way Reagan', in **New Socialist** (London) 21 November 1984, pages 17-22, on the implications of the Kissinger plan.

8. See discussion in Robinson and Norsworthy, pages 24-33.

9. See figures for El Salvador quoted in J Pearce, page 244, for example.

10. See the comments offered by secretary of state Rogers in **Foreign Affairs** (Washington) volume 63, number 3 (1985) pages 560-580.

11. See Arce's comments in Invernizzi and others, pages 14-16.

12. C Vilas, **The Sandinista Revolution** (New York 1986) page 109.

13. Vilas, page 109.

14. A fact of which it made great play in the document **What the present US administration does not want you to know about Nicaragua.**

15. See C Vilas, 'War and revolution in Nicaragua', in **Socialist Register 1987** (London 1988); also E Baumeister, 'The structure of Nicaraguan agriculture and the Sandinista agrarian reform', in Harris and Vilas (editors) **Nicaragua: A revolution under siege** (London 1985) pages 10-35.

16. See Vilas, **The Sandinista Revolution**.

Chapter 11: WHAT WENT WRONG?

1. Caraggio and Irvin, in **Nicaragua: A revolution under siege.**

2. Vilas, **The Sandinista Revolution**, page 109.

3. Nuñez and Burbach, **Fire in the Americas** (London 1989) page 14.

4. Nuñez and Burbach, page 44.

Appendix: REPORT FROM MANAGUA / Sabby Sagall

Thanks are due to Mike Gonzalez for useful information and advice, and to Oscar Lobos for help with translation.

1. Weber, page 53.

2. Economist Intelligence Unit, **Country Profile 1989-90: Nicaragua** (London 1989) page 14.

3. J Dunkerley, **Power in the Isthmus: A Political History of Modern Central America** (London 1988), pages 292-3.

4. Dunkerley, **Power in the Isthmus**, page 304; C Vilas, 'War and

Revolution in Nicaragua', in Miliband, Panitch and Saville (editors) **Socialist Register 1988** (London 1989) pages 191-6.

5. Vilas, in **Socialist Register 1988**, pages 197-8.

6. Economist Intelligence Unit, **Country Profile**, page 18; **Barricada Internacional**, special issue, February 1989, page 7.

7. Weber, page 89; Dunkerley, **Power in the Isthmus**, page 300.

8. Economist Intelligence Unit, **Country Profile**, page 22; **Barricada Internacional**, 3 June 1989, page 6.

9. Economist Intelligence Unit, **Country Profile**, page 17.

10. Economist Intelligence Unit, **Country Profile**, pages 15 and 26-27.

11. 'Economic Commission for Latin America' quoted in **Barricada Internacional**, 6 May 1989.

12. Vilas, in **Socialist Register 1988**, page 182; **Barricada Internacional**, 25 March 1989.

13. Economist Intelligence Unit, **Country Profile**, page 14.

14. Economist Intelligence Unit, **Country Profile**, page 17.

15. Economist Intelligence Unit, **Country Report number 2, 1989: Nicaragua**, (London 1989) pages 14 and 16.

16. **Barricada Internacional**, 20 May 1989, pages 9 and 11, and 17 June 1989, page 8.

17. Economist Intelligence Unit, **Country Report**, page 15, and **Country Profile**, page 26; **Barricada Internacional**, special issue, May 1989, page 6, and 25 February 1989, page 9.

18. **Barricada Internacional**, 11 February 1989, page 7.

19. **Barricada Internacional**, 20 May 1989, page 10.

20. **Barricada Internacional**, 17 June 1989, page 5; O Morales: 'The Crisis, Economic Policy and Nicaraguan Workers', in **Unidad Revolucionaria**, June 1989, pages 2-3.

21. See T Cliff, **Lenin 1917-1923: The revolution besieged** (Bookmarks, London 1987) chapters 7 and 9.

Other publications from Bookmarks

Revolutionary Rehearsals / *edited by Colin Barker*
Five times in the 20 years the working class took mass action: France 1968,
Chile 1972-3, Portugal 1974, Iran 1979 and Poland 1980-1. This book gives
the lie to those who say the working class is finished as a political force.
272 pages. *£4.95 / $9.50*

South Africa between Reform and Revolution / *Alex Callinicos*
The crisis of white rule in South Africa has been at the centre of world
attention since the popular upsurge of 1984. Only swingeing emergency
powers hold the regime in place. This analysis looks at the stregths and
weaknesses of both sides. 230 pages. *£4.95 / $8.50*

Revolution and Counter-revolution in Iran / *Phil Marshall*
From the oppression of the Shah to that of the Ayatollah—but why?
This book looks at the various forces acting during the Iranian revolution of
1979, particular the working class and the left. 128 pages. *£3.50 / $6.75*

Intifada / *Phil Marshall*
Following the mass uprising of Palestinians in Israel's occupied territories,
this book exposes the structure of domination of which Israel is the
keystone: an imperialism whose foundations lie in Britain 100 years ago
and the US today—and which oppresses workers all over the Middle East.
256 pages. *£5.95 / $11.00*

The Fire last time: 1968 and after / *Chris Harman*
The year 1968 was a political watershed: the May events in France, the
Prague Spring in Czechoslovakia, ghetoo risings in the US. This book looks
at the contradictions in the world system which led to these
upheavals—and how the system reasserted its control.
406 pages. *£6.95 / $13.50*

Israel: The Hijack State / *John Rose*
A brief outline of the history of Zionism and the state of Israel, showing the role that Israel plays in the world system as 'watchdog for the West'.
80 pages. *£2.50 / $4.75*

Ireland's permanent revolution / *Chris Bambery*
For over 200 years it has been the 'Irish problem'. This book looks behind the violence, at the religious discrimination and injustice that are its cause—and which are themselves but symptoms of a deeper, class divide.
128 pages. *£3.50 / $5.95*

Women and Perestroika / *Chanie Rosenberg*
Takes the changing situation for women in Russia—under the Tsar, Stalinism and today under Gorbachev—as a touchstone by which to judgeb the effects of perestroika on the lives of workers, women and men alike.
128 pages. *£3.95 / $7.50*

Bailing out the system / *Ian Birchall*
In 1945 an astute Tory politician told the British House of Commons: 'If you do not give the people reform, they are going to give you revolution.' Since then, reformism has again and again saved the capitalist system, defusing workers' struggle whenever it threatened to bring radical change.
304 pages. *£5.95 / $12.00*

The Quiet Revolutionary / *The autobiography of Margaret Dewar*
From schoolgirl in Petrograd during the 1917 revolution to become an opponent of both Stalinism and Nazism in the Germany of the 1930s —this is the story of one of the 'ordinary' people who are the real movers of history. 224 pages. *£5.95 / $12.50*

Available from bookshops, or by post from Bookmarks
(add 10 per cent to cover postage, minimum 35p or $1).

BOOKMARKS

265 Seven Sisters Road, Finsbury Park, London N4 2DE, England
PO Box 16085, Chicago, IL 60616, USA
GPO Box 1473N, Melbourne 3001, Australia

Bookmarks bookshop in London runs a large socialist mail order service. We have stocks of books and pamphlets from many publishers on socialism, internationalism, trade union struggle, women's issues, economics, working-class history, the Marxist classics and much, much more. We will send books anywhere in the world. Write for our latest booklists to:
BOOKMARKS, 265 Seven Sisters Road, London N4 2DE, England.